The Manager Trap

13 ½ Pitfalls to Avoid

The
Manager Trap

13 ½ Pitfalls to Avoid

HOWARD MILLER

Fulcrum Point
San Francisco

The Manager Trap: 13 ½ Pitfalls to Avoid
Published in the United States by
Fulcrum Point
30 Crestline Drive, Suite 2
San Francisco CA 94131
415-642-0843
www.fulcrumpointpartners.com

Copyright 2011 by Howard Miller.
2nd edition September, 2013

ISBN: 978-0-9843995-1-2

Printed in the United States of America

To my brother Andy

Thanks for helping me out of a few traps of my own throughout the years!

I'd like to thank the following people, who in one way or another, helped me to develop this book.

My sincere thanks to: Eric Ball, Ismael Barba, Nannette Rundle Carroll, Karen Gee, Paolo Miranda, Marian Mullally, Beth Proudfoot, Trudy Triner, Judith Wilson, and my parents, George & Lila Miller.

Thank you for your assistance, enthusiasm, support and encouragement!

Table of Contents

About this Book

Your job as a manager is tough. You must balance the needs of the company with the skills of the people who work for you. You may not agree with everything the company does. But since you represent the company, you might need to be optimistic or positive about objectives or policies you don't like or even understand.

You must manage conflict between your employees, and between different departments, while making sure company objectives are met.

You can easily blur the lines between the work you need to do and the capabilities of your employees.

Technology gives you access to more information, yet it increases the expectation of delivery.

HR laws have become stricter about what is acceptable and not acceptable.

Some of you have the challenges of employees who belong to unions, while some of you deal with employees who do just enough to get by or are counting the days to retirement.

If you are a new manager, you must adjust to significant changes in the way your contribution is perceived. Before you were a manager, your success was based on you and what you did. Now you need to rely on your team for your success, some of whom you may not like or even trust.

Actually, this applies to seasoned managers as well!

And just as it seems things are going smoothly, there is an emergency; something breaks down and you're picking up the pieces all over again.

A student in one of my management courses asked on the first morning of the course if there was one general lesson, one theme, to get out of the course. There was.

The lesson was how to juggle it all.

You start by asking yourself *What keeps me awake at night?* or, *What is my constant source of stress at work?*

If you can sleep better and/or have less stress, you will feel better. When you feel better, you will be of better service to your employees, your company, your friends, family and yourself.

That was the theme of the management course and that is the theme of this book. *This book is to help all managers avoid the top traps and pitfalls most managers fall into without realizing it.*

By understanding and doing any or a combination of the suggestions in this book, you can alleviate your stress and increase your productivity and the effectiveness of your team.

The word *dysfunctional* is often associated with families. The corporate culture has so much dysfunction it can make the issues in a family seem trite!

But this book is not about how to change the corporate culture you work in. Rather, it is about how you can work better within it. There are ideas for you to consider implementing or changing, and tools on how to get into action.

This book presents ideas and tools in an easy-to-understand format. Change can happen in an instant. It might take years to get to that instant, but it only takes an instant.

My hope is that this book will help you get to these instances.

Introduction

A man walks into a library and says to the librarian, *"I'd like a café latte and a blueberry scone."* The librarian gasped and said *"Sir, we're in a library."*

The man said *"Oh, I'm sorry."* Then in a low whisper, he said *"I'd like a café latte and a blueberry scone."*

Funny story, isn't it?

I was visiting my folks in Florida. They moved there from New York several years ago. A lot of friends from throughout their years live there. The average age is probably 80 years old.

I was at their pool without them and ran into one of their friends, Hilda. She was with three other women and they were all staring at me. To break up the silence, I decided to tell them that joke.

At the end of the joke, one of the women stared at me, and said in a serious tone with a thick New York accent, *"We can't get scones down here."*

Hilda turned to her and said *"No, Bernice. Oh, you're right; we can't get good scones down here."*

They then proceeded to have an in depth discussion about scones, the good places to get them in New York and the inadequate places in Florida. I was left standing there wondering what was going on!

How on earth did a joke turn into a serious discussion on scones? What got misinterpreted between my delivery and their comprehension?

I left thinking, well, they are older, and in their own world. This type of miscommunication couldn't possibly happen in the corporate world.

Ummm. Yes it can!

Do you ever find yourself in a conversation in an unexpected place while at work? Perhaps when you're walking down the hall, in the bathroom, or leaving the building? Then you find yourself with actions resulting from a conversation you didn't know you were going to have.

Or you know you're having a conversation, but perhaps you aren't as focused as you could be. You might be multitasking and your mind might be somewhere else.

Missing one word can change the entire meaning of a conversation!

In one of the management workshops I facilitate, I do an exercise similar to the telephone game we played as children. I ask for four volunteers. I send three of them from the room. With the remaining volunteer, I pretend I'm in a hurry and have to catch a cab. I relay information to her or him, just three or four pertinent points. I rush out.

Then I call another volunteer back into the room and have the first volunteer enact the same scenario with the second volunteer as I did with the first one. We repeat this with the remaining volunteers. By the end, 75% -90% of the original message is missing, key parts have been changed (such as names) and other things are made up.

And if any dramatic words or situations such as *alcohol, lay offs* or *catastrophic* are used, they are invariably carried to the end of the chain, but the way they are used at the end is mostly different than how they were used at the beginning!

It is so easy to have miscommunication because people are not listening or are not fully focused. For managers, this miscommunication can have great impact because they are responsible for the success of the team.

To get out of *The Manager Trap* and avoid pitfalls, managers should:

1. Be as objective as possible.
2. Implement coaching skills.
3. Focus on what matters and not on what can suck the life out of you!
4. Give effective feedback.
5. Delegate by the task and not by the person.
6. Know how to *motivate* your employees.

The 13 pitfalls are grouped under those themes.

The pitfalls under *Be as objective as possible* are:

1. Confusing subjective thoughts with facts.
2. Assuming we know what certain words mean.
3. Misusing acronyms.
4. Not understanding how your values can get in your way.
5. Saying "My door is always open."
6. "Difficult personalities"

The pitfalls under *Implement Coaching Skills* are:

7. Not listening.
8. Avoiding questions.
9. Engaging in employee's stories.

The pitfall under *Focus on what matters and not what can suck the life out of you!* is:

10. Dealing with *Focus vacuums.**

The pitfall under *Give effective feedback* is:

11. Not giving effective feedback. **

The pitfall under *Delegate by the task and not by the person* is:

12. Ineffective delegation.

The pitfall under *Know how to motivate your employee* is:

13. Attempting to motivate someone the way you want to be motivated

And the half pitfall:

Not being a **whole** manager who uses the skills mentioned in this book every day!

*Focus vacuums occur when we allow our attention to become focused on issues for which there is no constructive solution. These include the following:

- Generational differences.
- Absenteeism.
- Tardiness.
- Older employees.
- Employees who have more technical experience than you.
- Office gossip.
- Lazy employees.
- Employees who don't appear to be bright.
- Employees counting the days to retirement.
- Morale.
- "Red herrings."

**Reasons effective feedback isn't given:

- Not willing to take the time to give feedback.
- Having infrequent feedback sessions.
- Unclear understanding of the elements of effective feedback.

This book will go into detail about each of these themes so you can enhance your managerial skills and become aware of what you are consciously or unconsciously doing to minimize miscommunication.

Be as Objective as Possible

Being as objective as possible means looking at facts. What gets in the way of objectivity? Our own beliefs, values, perceptions and opinions. This is subjectivity.

Subjectivity is a pitfall because it disables us from stepping away from a difficult situation or person, and it prevents us from seeing the big picture. This can cause us endless stress, headaches, sleepless nights, arguments and miscommunication.

Because we are human, we will always have subjective thoughts. While it is ideal to aim for total objectivity, attaining it isn't humanly possible. But minimizing subjectivity, especially in difficult situations, will keep you and your employees on a path that can minimize unproductive time due to misunderstandings.

The overall pitfall is subjectivity. The solution is objectivity.

This pitfall impacts your ability to write up performance appraisals most efficiently and conduct productive and continuous feedback sessions with your employees. This pitfall can impact every conversation you have where there are negative subjective thoughts. It impacts your internal dialogue, which keeps you in the cycle of manager traps and pitfalls.

There are specific actions you can take in order to minimize subjectivity and shift to objectivity. But first, let's look at common subjectivity pitfalls.

Pitfall 1

Acting on your subjective thoughts as facts

Every day, you probably have thoughts about the people around you. For example, you may think Pamela is rude or Jeff is short tempered, or that you do not like Ted's attitude.

What you may not realize is that we often act on these *thoughts* as if there were *facts*. We use them as facts when we communicate with others; and we use them as measurements in our feedback sessions and performance reviews.

Consider how you might feel if someone told you he didn't like your attitude. What if someone told you that you appeared rude or abrupt at meetings? Or you weren't enthusiastic enough about your job?

You likely might feel confused, de-motivated and possibly angry.

These thoughts are only your opinions, they are not facts. Even if everyone holds the same opinion of a person, it doesn't make the opinion a fact.

When we treat our subjective thoughts as facts, we are creating an environment for misinterpretation, failed communication, confusion and de-motivation.

The byproducts of this type of environment are wasted hours, added stress, potential HR involvement; and in the extreme cases, legal action.

Subjective thoughts, left unchanged to objective facts, have even shown up in performance appraisals.

Some examples:

- Giving high ratings to those you like and lower ratings to those you don't like.
- Favoring long term employees by giving them the benefit of the doubt while withholding that benefit for employees with less seniority.
- Focusing the evaluation on what occurred most recently, instead of focusing on what has occurred during the entire evaluation period.

By becoming more objective and sticking to facts, you can minimize these management "gotchas."

But how do you become more objective and stick to facts?

First, you need to be aware. Be aware of the difference between what is subjective and what is objective.

When you recognize you are using subjectivity, you have already made progress. Many of us don't consciously realize what we're doing.

Once you recognize this, you need to decide if you're willing to shift the subjective to the objective. This is your personal choice.

If you are, there are a variety of tools that can help with the shifting process. They are discussed in this book.

The process of shifting from subjectivity to objectivity gets easier with practice, but it can be challenging. This is especially true when a situation or person provokes a strong clash with your internal, personal values. It is human and natural to find this difficult, but the situation can still be alleviated if you are willing to try.

But if you aren't, the situation will probably remain unresolved or worsen.

There is a common and overused subjective word. It contains 4-letters and begins with F.

What is this 4 letter word that managers should avoid?

After you get past the obvious gutter word, you might have thought of *fail*. I'm guessing this because when I ask this question of managers, most say *fail*.

But it's okay to *fail*. In fact, if you give your employees an environment where it's safe to fail, it increases their chance for success.

The four-letter word beginning with F to avoid is *fair*. Why?

Because *fair* is so subjective. What's fair to you is not fair to me.

When you engage in a conversation with an employee who claims something is not fair, you can never win. No matter how hard you try, it still may not seem fair to your employee.

And that's not fair!

But *fair* is a word used everywhere. It's used in political campaigns and in promises to promote goodwill; it's used as an attempt to build camaraderie and teamwork. The Academy of Management lists *fairness* as one of their 54 work values.

There is even a policy in the United States called the Fairness Doctrine. This was a policy of the United States Federal Communications Commission (FCC), introduced in 1949, that required the holders of broadcast licenses to present controversial issues of public importance *and* to do so in a manner that was, in the Commission's view, honest, equitable and balanced.

There is also the Unfairness Doctrine, which is a principle in United States trade regulation law. This doctrine allows the Federal Trade Commission (FTC) to declare a business practice *unfair* because it is oppressive or harmful to consumers, even though the practice is not an antitrust violation, an incipient antitrust violation, a violation of the *spirit* of the antitrust laws, or a deceptive practice.

There is even a website called *fairness.com* that gives advice about fairness matters and maintains profiles of almost 10,000 people, publications, and organizations involved in fairness issues while keeping up to date on important fairness topics.

Seems that *fair* is an important word in many different conversations in the world, so it's only natural for managers to use the word.

But engaging in conversation about fairness is a major indicator of the pitfall of acting on subjective thoughts as facts.

This is because what's fair to you may not seem fair to someone else.

Fairness is a feeling based on our values, experience and our past. It's not about being right or wrong. Yet, if we feel something is not fair, we do feel we are being wronged or that we're in the right.

Fair is subjective. Subjective measures and suggestions cannot lead to any agreement unless everyone involved sees the situation *exactly the same way*.

And no one sees anything exactly the same way.

Therefore, avoid the *f* word!

Literally and metaphorically.

Be as objective as you can be.

By doing so, you limit the subjective and minimize the pitfall of using subjectivity as facts.

Pitfall 2

Assuming what certain words mean

Another exercise I do in some of my management seminars is list common words on a flip chart or white board—words such as *frequently, occasionally, sometimes, always* and *never.*

I then ask everyone to write down any number between zero and 100 that quantifies what the word means to them when they hear it. For example, if someone says that they *frequently* go to these meetings, what number does *frequently* represent? We then do the same for each word in the list.

The results are always fascinating. The range of numbers will go from low to high on almost every word. The word *always* doesn't get 100 every time. There are people who apply a lower number based on their past experiences and their beliefs about the word.

The same applies to *never.* In fact, I only had one class in which everyone applied 100 for *always* and zero for *never.* And this was a class with fewer than 10 people. Not getting the variant scores in this class surprised me, based on the numerous times I had done this exercise in the past.

Now you may be thinking this is irrelevant. People will apply different numbers to everyday common words, but who is not going to understand what *always* or *never* means when used in a sentence?

Well, people will misinterpret—they hear what they want to hear.

A manager in one of my workshops told this story about the use of everyday words:

The manager had a problem employee. He increased his feedback to his employee, telling him if he didn't shape up, he'd be let go. The employee never improved. So one day, the manager called the employee into the room to tell him he was fired. The employee was shocked.

The manager was confused. He said to his employee, "*I told you if you didn't shape up, you'd be let go.*"

The employee's response: "*Yes, but you didn't say I'd be fired.*"

This employee was a blithering idiot, right? Well, maybe not. What else could *let go* mean?

Maybe the employee thought *I'd be let go to another department* or *I'd be let go to another position, I'd be made part time* or *I'll be let go and away from this manager I can't stand!*

Whether it was denial, ignorance or hearing what we want to hear, we have misinterpreted what has been said to us at one time or another.

And as managers, our best attempts to be clear can still lead to different conclusions than what we were communicating—even with the use of everyday words!

To avoid this pitfall and minimize miscommunication, try to be very specific and use measurable feedback. The less you leave open to interpretation, the less miscommunication will occur.

One word used the wrong way can mean the message you want to deliver is not received the way you wish.

We subjectively interpret common words, and subjectivity can lead to different conclusions for different people.

Pitfall 3

Acronyms

Acronyms can also be subjective. At first, this may not seem to make sense. After all, acronyms are abbreviations that are formed using the initials of a phrase or name.

The use of acronyms in the corporate world continues to increase, and some acronyms are used so often that we think we should know what they mean. Therefore, we guess we know what they mean, when it fact we aren't sure! An acronym for a technical term could have five different meanings to five different people.

There is a website that lists 68 corporate acronyms. I took a look at them. Some are obvious, such as *CEO* and *CFO*.

But what about *LIFO* and *FIFO*? If you're in IT or accounting, you would recognize those terms (*last in first out* and *first in first out*).

Have you ever been in a meeting with IT people who throw around the acronyms because they assume everyone knows what they mean? If you're not in IT, you might ask what they mean (unless it went right over your head). But if you think you should know, you won't ask.

But do they always mean the same thing?

The list of 68 corporate acronyms has *R* listed twice.

In one circumstance it means *retired* and in another it means *resigned*.

But when does it mean *retired* and when does it mean *resigned*?

I don't know!

And of course we all know what *IPO* stands for, don't we??!!

The point is, acronyms are based on assumed meaning---and assumptions and can lead to miscommunication.

This is a pitfall managers should avoid.

Communicate with full words.

Here is an exercise to decrease the chances of miscommunication using acronyms:

Put the acronyms on a list and email the list to everyone with whom you'll use it. Ask them to tell you what the acronym stands for. If everyone correctly understands an acronym, use it. If someone doesn't, tell them what it means.

If a significant number of people don't correctly understand the acronym, don't use the acronym!

Pitfall 4

Your values are subjective

According to the dictionary, the definition of *values* is *the quality (positive or negative) that renders something desirable or valuable* or *the degree of importance you give to something.*

Values are considered subjective, and they vary across people and cultures. Types of values include ethical/moral, doctrinal/ideological (political, religious), social and aesthetic.

Values evolve from interactions with the external world and can change over time. Values developed early in life may be resistant to change.

Values, which are *our personal truth,* do these things:

- Filter perceptions.
- Underlie actions, assumptions, and expectations.
- Always have a strong positive meaning for us.

Values impact our thinking, our behavior, and our beliefs. They can lead to a self-fulfilling prophesy. Often, others will behave as you expect them to according to your values.

Examples of values include diligence, paying attention to detail, integrity, honesty, professionalism, and fun, among many others.

Have there ever been times when you didn't adhere to one of your values?

For example, if you value honesty and/or integrity, do you ALWAYS (meaning 100% of the time!) act with honesty or integrity?

Most likely, the answer is no.

We are all human; therefore, we can make many, many mistakes. When we make these mistakes, we can be in conflict with our values. And often, when we make these mistakes, we are not accountable to anyone, so we can let them go unnoticed.

In other words, what we value we still sometimes won't do ourselves.

If this is true for us, is it true for others?

Understanding your own values and accepting that others have different values can help you recognize your subjectivity. When you can see your subjectivity, you are more able to move toward objectivity.

This is easier said than done.

When a belief touches our core, it becomes very personal. We may not recognize that something is not a fact, but our opinion.

Separating personal beliefs from managerial responsibilities can be so challenging that you may not undertake it until the costs to you personally have become steep.

Pitfall 5

"My door is always open."

President Barack Obama, when delivering a speech to a joint session of Congress, said:

"If you come to me with a serious set of proposals, I will be there to listen. My door is always open."

I'm sorry, but the president's door isn't always open. If it were, how could he get anything accomplished?

In fact, if you Google *Barack Obama my door is always open*, there are about 269,000 hits. I guess he says that expression a lot.

His door isn't always open. Neither is yours.

Yes, we know what you mean when you say it and you know what someone means when they say it to you. We think we know what they mean: that they are open to discussion and they seek open communication.

So why don't we start communicating more efficiently by making that statement a bit more accurate?

Your door is not always open. If you have a meeting going on, you don't want someone else walking in.

This kind of statement sets you up for failure because you are not able to keep your word. And not keeping your word leads to miscommunication, which is one of the biggest challenges for all managers.

When dealing with employees who need your guidance, it would be more meaningful to say something such as *"if you have any questions, email me anytime."* This gives them an avenue of support, but it does not imply a commitment from you to provide an immediate response.

This is a subtle yet effective way to say what you mean. It could lead to other expressions you say which might be more accurate if expressed a little differently.

Pitfall 6

Difficult personalities

Do you have employees who are difficult because they have difficult personalities? You may not say this aloud (good for you!), but you think it!

Try to stop using the word *personality* and use *behavior*.

Why? What's the difference?

The difference is that people can't change their personalities (unless they take drugs to help make the change or they have supernatural powers that enable them to change their personalities), but *everyone* can change their *behavior*.

If only one person changes behavior, it will change the dynamics between two people who are in conflict.

In 1968, Walter Mischel challenged the assumption that personality determined behavior, and instead claimed that a person's behavior is variable from situation to situation, depending on the situational circumstance.

Viewing behavior from the *situation* viewpoint means that behavior depends on the situation itself. But viewing behavior from the *personality* viewpoint means that behavior depends on characteristic personality styles and is consistently displayed without regard for the situation.

So as a manager, how can you correct or address a situation when you're thinking in terms of personality?

You can't.

But when you start thinking that a person's *behavior* is difficult, you can try to rectify the situation.

In some of my workshops, I include the subject *How to deal with difficult people*. All workshop participants are anxious to learn about this topic. I believe they hope to learn about an amazing tool that will change a difficult person and fix the problem.

That's one of the reasons I teach this on the last day of the seminar.

I have each manager do the following exercise:

- Think of someone who is difficult for you (we stick with work, not personal lives.)
- Put the person's name at the top of a page.
- Then create two columns as shown below.

Name of Difficult Person

What you say aloud	What you say to yourself

In the first column, write what you say to that person and in the second column, write what you say to yourself about that person

If you're being honest with yourself, most likely the right column is more negative in its tone.

Another reason I do this exercise on the last day of the seminar is because people are more comfortable with each other so they tend to be more honest about what they wrote.

For example, one manager was having trouble with an employee who was habitually late in delivering products. Using the exercise, the manager wrote:

Employee Who is Always Late Delivering Products

What you say aloud	What you say to yourself
What prevented you from getting this assignment in on time?	What the *! @* is wrong with you? A trained monkey could get these assignments done faster than you.
	I don't want to hear any more of your dumb excuses!

The question in the left column is actually a great question that can lead to opportunity and solutions. However, what's in the right column drives this situation.

After writing this exercise and talking about the situation with the class, the manager realized how his real/inner thoughts colored the interactions with his employee. He had no respect for his employee, and until he was willing to look at this differently, *it would never change.*

So the manager was contributing to make this situation difficult.

An example of what one manager wrote about their manager:

What you say aloud	What you say to yourself
	You're worthless.
	You're the worst manager I ever had.
	You couldn't lead a bunch of old ladies across the street without getting one killed.

This isn't a typo. The manager said *nothing* to his manager! Saying nothing might be perceived as better than yelling or being rude (which is probably true), but saying nothing can keep situations lingering and stale when they could be changed with a conversation.

Doing this exercise, you can start to take ownership of a situation where you are responsible or where you can create positive change by modifying your actions.

Avoiding the pitfall of *seeing others with difficult personalities* can be very challenging!

You may not want to do this.

One reason is *your situation may not be serious enough to look at it differently.*

Another reason is *it can serve us to keep thinking about someone as difficult, because it makes us right.*

The concept of difficult personalities is a subject that encompasses one's own values, spirituality and general attitudes about work and life ethics.

Usually these won't change unless a situation is severe enough to warrant the change.

But being able to shift from seeing someone with a difficult personality can lead to opportunities where they didn't previously exist.

Implementing Coaching Skills

There are many types of coaches working within corporations — executive coaches, management coaches, and business coaches. There are several coaching schools certified by the International Coaching Federation (ICF), including Coaches Training Institute (CTI), Coach University, and New Ventures West that provide education to coaches.

Coaching is its own profession, usually practiced by independent consultants. Some are exclusively coaches. Others, like me, do a combination of coaching, teaching, and facilitating.

The *trap* that occurs when managers implement coaching skills is seeing yourself as your employee's coach. You are not. You are an employee's manager. And as a manager, you sometimes need to have the final word because you have the ultimate responsibility for your team.

An outside coach has a very different relationship with an employee than a manager does. An employee might be more candid speaking with someone outside the company than with their own manager.

Although you are not a coach, you can still use coaching skills to be a more effective manager.

The coaching skills that managers can implement include:

- Listening more and talking less!
- Asking questions that lead to opportunity.
- Focusing on outcomes instead of employees' stories.

Coaching Skill 1

Listen more and talk less!

I was voted the most talkative senior in my high school. So I see the irony of telling managers they should listen more and talk less!

It takes confidence to talk less and listen more because it means that you trust and have faith in your employees to find the solutions they need. You are not in your own way when you do listen more and talk less.

The trap is doing most of the talking. This can be a difficult habit to break. Our corporate culture expects those who are in positions of authority to do the talking and to lead the conversation.

Especially when you are in a volatile situation with someone, leading the conversation isn't going to get to solutions. The exception to this is when a volatile situation involves threats---but to be more effective in any situation, start by letting the other person talk.

Listening is not easy. It takes effort.

In some of my management workshops, we do an exercise to practice and strengthen listening. I organize the class into groups of three. The team of three consists of a listener, a talker, and an observer, and everyone gets a chance to practice each role.

The talker speaks for approximately two to three minutes about a work situation.

The listener just listens---no note taking, and no questioning.

Howard Miller

Of course, in a real life situation you might take notes and ask questions. But that's not the focus of this exercise. It's simply to listen. The observer's role is to take notes and point out anything they observed, and then to facilitate a conversation following the three-minute period of talking.

After doing the exercise, participants observed the following:

- Listening isn't easy to do.
- There is an urge to ask questions.
- By just listening to everything a speaker has to say, some of those questions are answered even before they are asked.
- There is an impulse to take notes.
- It's easy to get distracted by outside noises, such as the email notification beep from your computer.
- You have to focus more intently to listen to a speaker who talks too quickly, or too slowly, or speaks with an accent.
- Listening takes a lot of energy. It's hard to do when your energy is low, or if you are tired or hungry.
- You have to focus more intently to listen to information about something you don't understand, or you find boring.
- It's hard to keep quiet and listen when you KNOW the solution.

There are several tips you can use to improve your listening skills. Most people don't try to enhance these skills. They don't even think about it.

Becoming conscious about listening more and talking less can make a difference to your success as a manager.

Other tips to enhance listening include:

- Turning away from your computer and phone while talking to someone.
- Coming up with a time—90 seconds or two minutes—when you consciously decide to let the other person talk without interrupting.
- Putting a finger over your mouth to remember to wait a bit before you speak.
- Remembering that *listening is your job.*

Coaching Skill 2

Asking questions that lead to opportunity

Asking questions is one of the most powerful communication tools we have. Why? A question has the potential to change the entire direction of a conversation, either positively or negatively.

The goal of a manager is to ask questions that lead to opportunities and solutions.

When should we be asking questions?

- To get clarification on a topic.
- To get more information.
- To show interest.
- To help development and growth.

But too often we ask questions that put our employees on the defensive. We may not mean to do this, but sometimes we use words or tones that create the wrong effect. Their answers will not usually lead to any enlightenment.

I wish there were an exact method to teach people to ask better questions that lead to opportunity.

There isn't, but there are some available guidelines:

- Ask less focused questions. These allow your employee to develop answers that aren't constricted by the structure of the question. For example, asking, *"What will you do differently?"* might result in broader answers than asking, *"What will you do differently to ensure more accuracy with the sales report?"*

- Avoid starting a question with the word *why*. It comes across as threatening. Instead, use *what* or *how*.

- Use the phrase W*hat prevented you*. You can use it in questions such as:
  - *What prevented you from completing the assignment?*
  - *What prevented you from meeting the objectives?*
  These questions are more compassionate than *Why didn't you complete the assignment? Or Why didn't you meet the objectives?*

- Dare to ask ineffective questions. The power is in figuring out when they are ineffective so you can ask new ones.

  - Questions are ineffective when they aren't leading to opportunity or solutions. If you ask a question that doesn't have viable answers, it's not because there aren't any. It's because it's a bad question! Ask another question.

The key is *to know when to change the question.*

It takes practice. The more you ask questions the more experience you'll get asking ones which work and ones which don't.

What can be frustrating (or exciting, depending how you look at it!) is that the same question can work in one situation and not in another.

There are times when I'm coaching a client and I ask a question. If I see that the question isn't leading to viable solutions or opportunities, I will interrupt and say, *"Forget it."* Then I ask it a different way.

This takes practice and the willingness to try and fail.

There are no guaranteed perfect questions!

I was coaching an executive at one time who was in charge of a group that faced a significant decision. The manager knew that most of the group would have to relocate in order to keep their jobs, and he knew most would not do it.

He was very frustrated and he asked me, *"How do I keep morale high when they know they are going to lose their jobs?"*

My response was, *"I have no idea. If we figure this out, let's write a book and get on Oprah!"*

I don't think he was expecting that response. He was expecting an answer to his question.

But what kind of answer is there? He's an executive, which means he must be pretty bright – if he can't come up with an answer, why should I?

Yes, I'm bright too, but the question doesn't have an answer.

This is because *it's not a good question.*

I asked him what he wanted. The executive wanted his staff to continue doing their work.

Together we came up with a question. *How do you support your staff finding other jobs while continuing to do their work?*

This question presents a different set of alternative solutions. We removed the problem of morale and created a different perspective.

Questions that don't have any kind of answers with opportunities are not good questions.

The *trap* for managers is asking questions that don't have viable solutions.

The *solution* is the ability to change the question.

Coaching Skill 3

Focus on the outcome and do not engage in the stories of the employee

In coaching terms, not engaging in the stories of the coached employee means not exploring the *why* and *what happened* in the past. A therapist does that. A coach doesn't.

It also means not engaging the excuses an employee presents when not meeting expectations. *Many times managers will respond to an employee's excuses and get diverted from the goal.*

Using your coaching skills means focusing on solutions.

Don't focus on what went wrong, but on how we can prevent it from happening again. Most of the time, managers ask what happened with the intention to help, but it puts their employees on the defensive.

This requires you to think before you talk to your employee. What do you want? What is the goal? If you focus on the goal when listening and asking questions, you avoid the subjectivity that can waste countless hours.

Using coaching skills requires you to be objective, to listen, and to ask questions that lead to opportunity. It means examining behaviors instead of personalities.

When you combine these skills, they can help you increase your capabilities as a manager.

Focus on What Matters and Not on What Can Suck the Life Out of You!

Managers are so focused on expected outcomes they don't realize their biggest obstacles are themselves.

One of the biggest challenges is even recognizing when you're in your own way, which could mean you are stuck in a *focus vacuum*.

What is a *focus vacuum*?

A vacuum is space that is entirely without matter. It is emptiness or a void. *Focus* means attention is drawn to this emptiness.

Managers can pay attention to issues that lead nowhere and take lots of time. These are the *focus vacuums* that lead to manager traps and pitfalls.

Some examples of focus vacuums are:

1. Generational issues.
2. Absenteeism.
3. Tardiness.
4. Dealing with employees who are older than you.
5. Employees who have more technical experience than you.
6. Gossip.

Let's examine each of these focus vacuums.

Focus Vacuum 1

Generational issues

I know I'm not going to make friends with everyone who has written articles and books on how to deal with different generations. A lot has been written about the issues between younger and older workers. Younger people feel entitled while older people are unwilling to change.

Dealing with *Generation X, Generation Y,* and *Baby Boomers,* has created many discussions because issues do exist.

But addressing issues for an entire group rather than for an individual is a focus vacuum.

If you Google *dealing with different generations at work* you will get approximately 9.2 million hits! Clearly this topic has been intensely researched and discussed.

The Huffington Post states that members of Gen Y are considered lazy. Interesting enough, they are the first generation not to list work ethic as a defining ethic. Therefore, we need to ask the following questions before coming to the conclusion that they are lazy:

- How does Gen Y understand work?
- What is their definition of work ethic?
- How does their understanding of work affect how and when Gen Y members produce results?
- How can employers collaborate with Gen Y to redefine the workplace?

This is a good start but I would go further to say get rid of the theory! Why separate Gen Y from any other generation?. Change those questions to:

- How does my *employee* understand work?
- *What is their definition of work ethic?*
- How does their understanding of work affect how and when *they* produce results?
- How can *my employee* collaborate with *their peers* to redefine the workplace?

In other words, there are people who do and do not fit stereotypes. It doesn't serve you to approach managing an employee based on age. Stop focusing on age and focus on the employee's results.

Focus Vacuum 2

Absenteeism

It is frustrating for a manager when an employee often calls in sick, especially on Mondays or Fridays! You know they're not sick, but can't take action because they are within the company guidelines.

It's natural to feel frustration. Absenteeism may conflict with your work values or your personal values.

This is one of the most common and damaging focus vacuums.

Organizations are paying a high price for absenteeism when they have to hire and train replacement employees. If your organization faces a high level of absenteeism, there is something wrong with your organization.

In order to reduce high levels of absenteeism, companies must identify organizational and individual factors that influence the high cost of absenteeism.

This is the responsibility of the company. You are the manager, not the company.

Do you have a responsibility to the company? Of course you do.

But if changing the level of absenteeism is not within your control, you add to the high cost of absenteeism by focusing too much on the issue. If you cannot create solutions, this causes added stress and frustration. What do you do about it?

Focus on what you can change and that would be your employee's productivity. Is the work being completed?

If the work is getting done, is there really a problem or is the absenteeism just bothering you?

If the work is incomplete, what should you do as a manager? Focus on the work and not on the belief that more work would be completed if the employee weren't absent.

Shift your focus from absenteeism to what must be accomplished.

Focus Vacuum 3

Tardiness

The issues surrounding tardiness are similar to the issues around absenteeism.

Some employees who must be at work precisely on time. But the majority of employees can arrive to work within a range of time without detracting from their work.

In one of my workshops, I had several managers tell me they get frustrated when they work long hours and their own manager feel they could work even more. This de-motivates them and creates a distance and lack of trust between them and their managers. Distrust generates thoughts that are negative and unproductive.

Do you want to be this kind of manager to your employees?

When employees come to work late, it's usually your issue. You are understandably annoyed. But your reaction is getting in your own way.

Again, focus on measurable objectives. Do not mention tardiness in regular feedback sessions. Focus on objectives not being met and see what the employee suggests to achieve a satisfactory level of performance.

Focus Vacuum 4

Dealing with employees who are older than you

I have had a lot of young managers (and what is young? Certainly that number is different depending on your own age!) in manager workshops with concerns about dealing with older employees. They soon realize this is their issue, and they are getting in their own way.

It's a lack of confidence within them, which is natural and normal considering the new responsibilities they have.

According to Employment Digest, a 2004 study for the Society for Human Resources Management found that keeping workers of different generations apart was not a successful business practice. Combined training, mentoring, collaboration and team-building activities helped, but communicating information in multiple ways proved most successful in managing multiple generations.

When you realize that focusing on age is a trap with no solution, you are free to refocus and look for objective measurements to measure the performance of each employee.

Gain respect and confidence by doing a great job!

Focus Vacuum 5

Dealing with employees who have more technical experience than you

True or false: you need to have technical experience to manage a technical group.

The answer is false.

As a manager your job is to support your employees and make them as successful as they can be so that you are successful as well. You do this by giving them what they need. You give them what they need by meeting with them regularly and creating environments where there are solutions created to obstacles that get in their way.

Those are the technical skills you need: the ability to meet with your employees, ask questions and listen to their answers, and help them create solutions.

If you don't have those skills, technical expertise might give you credibility with your employees, but it will not serve them fully.

In a prior life I taught financial software.

Although I had no knowledge of finance, I was hired because I had experience in training and in software applications, I got the job. I took a high level, one-day Finance course (something like "Finance for Dummies") and then I had to learn the software and teach it within a few weeks of being hired.

I remember the first time I was asked by a student *"Why would I use a journal?"*

I didn't have a clue.

So what did I do?

I turned to the class and asked them *"Why would any of you use a journal?"*

I got a couple of answers. So the next time I taught I had a couple of more answers and when I asked the class again I got even more answers.

Eventually I became pretty knowledgeable about finance so I was able to point out to *financial analysts* finance errors they were making while learning the software!

I even taught a more detailed budgeting/planning course. This subject took a little longer to comprehend, but by asking questions I was able to learn.

Okay, so I did this not as a manager.

But if you begin a technical job with a non-technical background and are able to succeed, couldn't you also do this as a manger?

In fact, it was at this job I had one of the best managers I ever had in my career. She knew nothing about finance or software yet she was a manager of instructors who taught financial software.

Why was she one of the best managers I ever had?

Because she asked questions and supported me. She didn't have the technical knowledge; what she did was talk with me to understand the situations and help brainstorm on solutions.

Focus Vacuum 6

Gossip

The odds are against you when you get the problem employee as one of your employees. You know the one; a man or woman who has been around the company for years, but no one can seem to get rid of them. They have a reputation, and now they work for you!

The common trap to fall into is listening to this history, which in fact is gossip.

Even if it's not malicious, office gossip kills camaraderie and morale. *It's also a way for teams to avoid holding difficult conversations.*

To fuel this gossip, the worst thing you can do is look at their old HR files. You're already biased against this person based on the gossip and now you'll have "facts" to back it up.

Unless they are already on probation, you are starting over with this person. Why not make it a clean slate? If they are measured against specific and measureable goals, you can ignore the gossip and focus on objective measurements. Maybe this person will not live up to these measurements; but just maybe they never got the opportunity to do so in the past because they didn't have a manager who met with them and supported them.

You could be this manager.

All of these focus vacuums have the potential to be wonderful opportunities for you. If you can recognize them as focus vacuums and as traps, then you can shift to solutions.

The solutions are simple yet complicated. To exchange all or most of the technical skills you have used up until now (and that have made you successful) for new, and likely untrained skills, can be daunting.

But *not* shifting from our focus vacuums keeps us focusing on situations which lead to no solutions.

Therefore, we would stay stuck in focus vacuums.

Give Effective Feedback

When writing challenges they face, several managers wrote *I didn't sign up to be a babysitter!*

According to the Merriam-Webster dictionary, the definition of a babysitter is "a person who cares for children usually during a short absence of the parents."

So you are correct; you didn't sign up to be a babysitter (although you are probably being paid much more than a typical babysitter!)

When I asked these managers what they meant by this statement, they felt they were spending too much time with some of their employees. They seemed to have to repeat the same thing over and over. Others managers felt they had to monitor their employees constantly, otherwise they would slack off.

Actually, this is your job.

When you accept that regular feedback is part of your job, you'll find that your conversations won't always be about their slacking off. Your relationship with each employee will build, and each relationship will have its own dynamics.

To give effective feedback you need to:

- Be willing to take the time to give feedback.
- Conduct regular feedback sessions.
- Know the elements of effective feedback.

In our corporate cultures, the annual performance review is the reflection of feedback between you and your employee.

Have you ever been unpleasantly surprised at an appraisal from one of your managers? How did it make you feel? You likely felt angry, unmotivated, and distrustful of your manager.

You don't want your employees to say they have been unpleasantly surprised by a performance appraisal that you conduct!

There should be no surprises come appraisal time. In fact, the meeting to sign the appraisal should be a mere formality where you both sign the form. The goal is to have no surprises.

How do you achieve this?

- Be willing to take the time to give feedback.
- Conduct regular feedback sessions.
- Know the elements of effective feedback.

Same bullet points as above!

So what are the traps for each of these items? And what are the solutions?

Feedback element 1

Be willing to take the time to give feedback

If you aren't willing to change your priorities and the way you view time so you will take time to give feedback, then even becoming fluent in the elements of effective feedback and understanding its importance won't help.

Blocking time on your schedule for your employees is crucial. Yes, there could be emergencies once in awhile. But on a regular basis, preferably weekly, taking time for *each* employee will build a foundation to avert traps many managers fall into.

While giving feedback may not be *urgent*, it is *important*. Start to recognize the need to do important work which isn't urgent. This recognition might increase your willingness to take the time to give feedback.

Feedback element 2

Conduct regular feedback sessions

Are feedback sessions where nothing changes better than having none at all?

That's an excuse some managers use. *Why bother? They've tried everything but nothing changed.* I tend to think they haven't tried everything, just the same thing over and over again!

Of course, there is also another excuse: *meeting regularly takes too much time,* or *we started meeting regularly but it became less frequent over time and then stopped.*

What kind of message does it send to your employees when these meetings stop?

Decades ago, I worked at IBM. This was a time when I didn't really need permission to obtain training. I just signed up for it and attended the course. There was a project management course in the middle of New York City. Rumor had it that much of the class had nothing to do with project management.

And it was true. The morning session was about project management, taught by a traditional long-term IBM employee. But the afternoon session was taught by someone who was so unlike the IBM culture of the time, and it was positively refreshing.

He challenged the process of promoting technical people into management roles that required interpersonal skills they didn't have. He challenged the validity of IBM marketing sales training. He also challenged the motives of some individuals. He asked one student whether his family or his job was most important. The guy said his family. The instructor then asked him what he would do if IBM offered him a promotion to a city where his wife didn't want to live. He said he would try to get his wife to see the benefits of moving. The instructor then told him he just lied. His job was most important because if it weren't, he would turn down the promotion because his wife didn't want to move.

All this honesty was much more than what we were used to within the IBM culture. It inspired one person to talk about his manager giving him a bonus under the table. Others talked about personal things they never thought they would discuss in a professional setting.

The instructor had a theme for his afternoon sessions. He asked what percentage of responsibility we thought we should have in any relationship. Most of us said 50%. He said *"No, you should be 100% responsible for any relationship---with a spouse, an employee or your own manager."*

Decades later, I still remember this piece of advice. I used it all the time as an employee. If I wanted feedback on my performance, I wouldn't wait for my manager to come to me. I would schedule a meeting. I didn't focus on whether my manager gave me consistent feedback because I took responsibility for obtaining feedback when I needed it.

What would it be like if each of your employee's took responsibility for ongoing continuous feedback from you?

If you see that it could make your life easier, you are on track to providing continuous feedback to each employee.

By initially taking responsibility of setting up and conducting regular feedback sessions, you are showing your intentions and displaying the importance of communication. In time (some faster than others), your employees will take responsibility as well.

But if you see this as something that would cause many interruptions in your day, I encourage you to look again.

If you meet regularly with your employees you will end up being more productive, feel more in control of your time, and have a greater impact on your team.

Start by taking 100% of the responsibility for each employee relationship. Keep your employees as your #1 priority. Conduct meetings on a regular basis.

Feedback element 3

Know the elements of effective feedback

Congratulations if you conduct regular meetings with your employees! This is a great step towards achieving more constructive communication and avoiding a lot of manager traps.

It's important to focus on the *effectiveness* of these meetings.

To be effective, you should:

- Develop an agenda for your meetings.
- Exercise the characteristics of effective feedback.

Develop an agenda for your meetings

Quality of meetings is important for managers and non-managers. Close to 100% of people who attend meetings say that at least half of the meeting was a waste of time. The underlying reason for this is the lack of an agenda, or an agenda that isn't followed.

Even though you meet one-on-one with your employee, it's still a meeting. Here is a sample agenda for ongoing one-on-one meetings:

Activity	Person Responsible
Employee says what's going well	Employee
Employee says what roadblocks they have	Employee
Employee tells you where they want your support	Employee
Discuss how support will be given	Both
Bring up anything that hasn't already been brought up	Manager
End by giving praise	Manager

You'll notice who drives the meeting and is doing more of the talking – not you! You are listening more and talking less.

All topics do not have to be covered in every meeting, but the agenda serves as a template.

Exercise the characteristics of effective feedback

There are five Fs in giving effective feedback.

Factual – As discussed, feedback should be objective. Stick to facts as often as possible. Convert subjective thoughts to objective facts. If you can't, think about whether this is something that you need to discuss with your employee.

Focused – Do not cover too many items at once. There might be an underlying theme (for example, missing several deadlines) but focus on one item at a time. Grouping them together might create inaccurate assumptions. Plus, it could overwhelm someone and cause them to miss important points.

Fast – Don't wait a long time to give either positive or constructive feedback. However, if you are angry or upset, wait until you're in a better frame of mind before giving feedback.

Frequently – This is a subjective term, but if you are having weekly meetings with each employee, that is sufficient frequency for giving feedback.

Freely – How comfortable are you giving praise to your employee? How comfortable are you giving constructive feedback? If you're uncomfortable, the way to make it easier is to start doing it on a regular basis.

I had a client who was an executive director at a non-profit. He had received feedback that he didn't communicate enough with his staff. We created a goal where he needed to give positive and constructive feedback at least once a week to someone on his staff.

The purpose of these actions was two-fold: it was to prepare him to conduct regular meetings with each employee, and to provide him with practice at giving feedback.

If you are not comfortable giving feedback, your employees will not be comfortable receiving feedback.

The only way to get past this is to practice giving feedback over and over again.

Delegate by the task and not the person

Delegation – a trap and a solution

Most managers do not delegate as much as they should, saying to themselves:

- There's not enough time to delegate
- It's easier to do it myself
- No one can do it as well as I can so I might as well do it myself
- I have non-managerial tasks I have to do that I can't delegate
- Things go wrong when I delegate.

Those are the common excuses managers give as to why they don't delegate. Do they sound familiar?

The *trap* with delegation is the excuses above.

The *solution* with delegation is doing it efficiently.

Think about this: what do executives spend their day doing? They attend meetings and they delegate.

If you wish to climb the management ladder, why not start delegating now so you know the best methods of delegation?

If that question doesn't grab you, here's another one: what's your job as a manager? Isn't it to grow your people to make them as successful as they can be?

Delegation is your responsibility. It's vital to your job.

From the excuses written:

- There's not enough time to delegate.
- It's easier to do it myself.
- No one can do it as well as I can so I might as well do it myself.
- I have non-managerial tasks I have to do that I can't delegate.
- Things go wrong when I delegate.

Which one if corrected would make the others easier?

It's the last one: *things go wrong when I delegate.*

If things didn't go wrong you would find your time freeing up so you could do other things, and you would find others could do it as well or better than you.

That last sentence might rub you the wrong way -- someone doing it better?!

If you choose to not delegate because you enjoy the work or you want to stay technically relevant to be marketable in the economy, that's your decision. Who can blame you? But this decision from a management perspective decreases your effectiveness and increases traps for you to fall into.

If you truly have tasks to do where you were told no one else can do them, then you shouldn't delegate those tasks. Also, if your staff is working to its fullest and are all overburdened, delegating under these circumstances might not be a motivator.

However, at least 90% of managers could delegate more.

So how can you minimize things going wrong when you delegate?

They are several methods and tools of delegation – a very successful one is Ken Blanchard's Situational Leadership II. This method has been implemented company wide at several corporations.

You probably don't have the ability to create company wide policy. But there are aspects of this method that you can implement.

The key to delegation – the most important ingredient to its success – is to know what you are delegating and to know the outcome or outcomes you desire.

Have you ever been delegated something where the outcome was unclear? It's very frustrating; you can spend countless hours thinking you are productive when that particular work is not needed.

Don't be a manager who isn't clear about what you are delegating!!

This is the biggest trap: not spending the time figuring out what you want. You can use any method of delegation, but if you don't have specific and measurable outcomes, everything is built on a house of cards. You might follow parts of a delegation process, but it will be unsuccessful without specific and measurable outcomes.

How do you figure out what specifically you need?

There are several ways:

- Write the outcomes that you want.
- Say them aloud.
- Discuss them with a peer or your manager.
- Discuss them with the person who will get the delegation assignment.

These conversations will help you focus on your objectives and outcomes.

After you have figured out the outcomes, you should determine the *importance* and the *urgency* of this project. Not everything needs to be done immediately. Conveying this to the person to whom you are delegating the project will help set their priorities.

Here is the next key to effective delegation: most of the time when we delegate, we simply hand the project over to the person. But often, you still need to be involved to some capacity.

Situational Leadership II emphasizes four different styles to use when delegating a project.

What it comes down to is:

- Technical competence *to do this project.*
- Motivation *to do this project.*

The words *to do this project* are emphasized above and doubly emphasized is the word *this*.

This is because delegation is project/outcome based. It's not thinking *I have senior employee so they know everything,* or, *this person is always willing to take things on.*

You need to look at it on a project by project basis because it can be different.

For example, your senior technician might know everything on the current system but if a new release comes out, she might need training. Someone else might be highly motivated until he hits a rough patch in his personal or professional life when he temporarily lacks the capacity to do more.

If the person to whom you are delegating needs technical guidance, you need to provide it – you may not be the one but you need to provide the person with the proper training or instruct someone else to train them.

If the person needs motivation to do the project, you will need to spend time on a regular basis to help them stay on track.

Situational Leadership lays out specific steps you can do to ensure success.

But the trap you need to avoid is just handing over a project.

The solution is to make sure the project you are delegating has these characteristics:

- A well defined goal that is specific and measurable
- A commitment from you to provide the "right" amount of time based on the employee's needs. You should always spend time with your employee, but you might need to spend more time if she needs motivation and encouragement and/or training. This can mean either the time to train her or the time to coordinate the training.

Know how to *motivate* your employees

I want my employees to want what I want: The traps of motivation and how to avoid them

There are numerous theories about how to motivate. The reality about motivation:

- It's not easy to motivate someone.
- For motivation to work, consequences (reward or punishment) must exist and must be implemented.
- Motivation requires ongoing feedback between you and your employee.

And hardest of them all:

- You must be able to remove your feelings about how you like to be motivated because your preferences won't work for everyone!

It's not easy to motivate someone

In some of my management workshops I play an opening game. I have each table act as a team. I assign them each a question (such as *what are the qualities of a great manager?* or *what do you want to get out of this workshop?*). Their objective is to get the answers from the other teams. What usually happens in the room is chaos! People want the other teams to remain at their respective tables so they can get input from them. Of course no one does; they all have their own objectives. So everyone is running after everyone!

It's the same with motivation. We want people to be motivated by the same things that motivate us. If they're not, we want to force them to be!!

But it doesn't work that way.

Motivating someone involves understanding their motivators, not yours.

To get motivation to work, there must be consequences

If one of your employees isn't doing something you need them to do, and there is no consequence of their inactivity, why should they do it? Clearly they don't want to, so why should they bother?

I have had many managers complain about their employees. When I ask them how they were evaluated usually they were evaluated as good to excellent!! Why would an employee change if there are no repercussions or rewards?

You can't give an employee a yearly appraisal of 4 or 5 (where 4 means Good and 5 means Excellent) if they are doing average work. They should get a 3. And if they're below average then they should get a 2!

But most managers are hesitant to give such a low rating. The main reason: we associate a 5 with an "A" in school, 4 as a "B" and 3 as a "C." And we don't want Cs!

Thinking this way keeps us from giving consequences to actions not completed.

There may be many reasons an employee isn't doing something you need them to do. It could be they aren't aware it needs to be done. That's easy to fix! But if it isn't easy to fix, it goes beyond a lack of awareness; they aren't motivated to do the task at hand. They are even comfortable hearing from you time after time about it not getting done.

The key is to get them uncomfortable.

What's the importance of the task that needs to be done? What happens if it's not done? What happens if it is done?

You need to figure out what you can offer as a reward or consequence. But if you aren't willing to follow through, do not use consequences as bait. If you do, your words are just that – words. If you promised a reward but did not deliver it, you have broken trust. If it's a consequence you didn't keep, then discipline will be even harder in the future.

You need to figure out the value of the project and identify a reward or consequence that you can follow through on.

Motivation requires ongoing feedback between you and your employee

Feedback was discussed earlier in the book. Ongoing feedback is the lifeline between a manager and their employee. When you have ongoing feedback you will get to know your employee better, and understand what does and does not motivate them.

When you have a project you need them to do and you know they aren't enthusiastic about the project, you will be better equipped to directly communicate your need for them to do it anyway. The bond and trust you have developed will make it more likely that the project gets done, if only because your employee knows they will have to provide project status in your regular meetings!

You must be able to remove your feelings about how you like to be motivated because your preferences won't work for everyone!

Classic motivational focusing traps:

- What if my employee is lazy or not bright?
- Motivating retiring employees.
- Morale.
- Red Herrings.

What if my employee is lazy or not bright?

There are other adjectives we can use besides lazy or not bright (i.e. they don't care, stupid, unenergetic, etc).

The overall point is how can you motivate someone if you feel a certain way about them? It will underline every conversation you have with them.

This is one of those focuses where *you* need to do work to make this relationship better.

What I've had managers do is to challenge their focus thought by writing things which contradict. For example, if a manager felt an employee was lazy I would challenge them to write 5 ways they were NOT lazy (whatever lazy meant to the manager). If they couldn't come up with five things, then write three things. If not three, can the manager come up with one thing?!

If you can get something in writing that challenges your thoughts, you have something to reference when your thoughts go towards you default.

It works for your thoughts about someone who is not bright – name one to five things they have done well.

But most important – you have to be motivated to want to do this!! You might enjoy thinking negatively about your employee (no, you aren't a terrible person, you are only human!) But if you need something done and you can get towards it by changing your focus, that may motivate you to do so.

Motivating retiring employees

A few managers in my workshops really want to know how to motivate retiring individuals who never go above or beyond the minimum requirements of their job.

How can a manager motivate this person?

Not a great question.

Put yourself in your employee's shoes. If you were ready to retire and were pretty secure in your job, how hard would you want to work?

You can ask the almost-retired employee to teach others what they do. If this doesn't work, you can ask what motivates them, but if nothing changes shift your focus to your other employees. Otherwise you are wasting time and detracting from employees who want to grow.

Howard Miller

Morale

When I tell managers to ignore tardy or absent employees, they push back saying that the rest of the team complains and morale goes down. The team doesn't think it is fair (there's that word again!) that one person can come and go as they please.

If you shift from this focus vacuum of <u>morale</u>, it can be a wonderful opportunity!

Remember, focusing on what is fair will not get you anywhere and neither will focusing on what you can't change. This also applies to the team. The best course of action when one or more of your employees complains about another employee is refocusing attention on them. Support the employee's concern, and then refocus them on their objectives.

It is easy to focus on the employee who is absent or tardy. This can bond the rest of the group because they all have a common thorn in their side. But the wasted time and energy in discussing this deflates morale and widens the gap of effective communication.

As a manager, you can increase opportunities for your other employees while figuring out the best course of action for the problem employee.

This can only happen if you shift your focus and avoid falling into the morale trap.

Red Herrings

"Red herrings" are observations that will obstruct in the creation of effective motivational strategies. They don't help lead to solutions. They might be actual issues, but they are superfluous to solving the problem at hand.

All the focusing traps above are red herrings.

Another example:

A manager in a workshop had the following situation:

She managed an employee who was an administrative assistant supporting two different directors. The manager was not a director. One of the directors liked the administrative assistant, but the other director wanted him fired as soon as possible.

The manager's opinion of the admin aligned with the director who wanted the admin fired, because she had evidence documenting that the admin hadn't met objectives for a long period of time.

This manager was confused about what to do because the directors had different opinions.

Red herrings – the directors' opinions – were the source of the manager's confusion. Both directors' opinions were irrelevant because the manager already had an opinion based on factual evidence.

In these situations, a manager should follow her own conclusions despite the differing views of others. A manager keeps a documentation trail, and evidence supports your actions.

Being able to stay focused and not be diverted by red herrings can save managers an immense amount of time, stress and frustration.

You must ignore what motivates you because your preferences won't work for everyone

This is a strong statement.

If you consciously or unconsciously believe other people are motivated by the same things that motivate you, you won't be able to motivate anyone who disagrees with you. Oh, you may be able to motivate some people for a short period of time, but not for the long haul.

Furthermore, if you can't remove your feelings and personal preferences, your reasons for attempting to motivate someone may not be serving the best interests of your employee or the company.

They may only be serving you.

Ouch!

You might feel your employee needs to be motivated because she isn't doing something and this personally bothers you. This happens. But is it self serving?

There are two ways to determine this:

Change your subjective thoughts about the situation to objective observations. If you cannot do this, your attempts to motivate her to change could very well be self serving.

Accept her behavior or empathize with his viewpoint. If you can't get to acceptance or empathy, your attempt to motivate change could also be self serving.

It takes courage to realize that in some situations, the best way to motivate another might be simply to drop the issue, because the issue is yours.

When you can do this, you are acting as a very confident manager!

General guidelines to help motivate

- Understand YOUR intention – are you trying to motivate using any of the classic motivational focus traps?
- Analyze your intentions – do you need to be proven right?
- Do you need to shift your focus?
- Do you need to identify the red herrings so you can more clearly create a motivational atmosphere?
- Include discussions of motivators in your regular meetings can help you understand what motivates your employees.
- Document everything to gather facts.

Creating an environment where your employees are self motivated, or where you motivate them, requires time from you to meet with your employees and understand their perspectives. But the time spent can very well get you the results you want, although the motivators that bring success for the team might be different from the motivators you would choose for yourself!

Management Toolbox

We've looked at six themes which emphasize the manager trap.

They are:

- Be as objective as possible.
- Implement coaching skills for managers.
- Focus on what matters and not what can suck the life out of you!
- Give effective feedback.
- Delegate as much as possible.
- Know how to *motivate* your employees.

Awareness of these themes can be enough to shift our actions to avoid the manager trap.

But there are also specific tools one can use which will help. There isn't one tool for one specific trap. Any of these tools can help in different situations.

Toolbox Overview

- Creating goals.
- The two questions for examining behavior.
- Five parts to a complete message.
- How to increase listening.
- Asking questions which lead to solutions.

Tool 1: Creating goals

When you have ambiguous goals, subjectivity takes over. If you look favorably at someone, all is fine (no one argues when they get compliments!). If you look unfavorably at them, you have problems!

The trick is to turn these subjective opinions, derived from the common traps, into an objective fact.

Not that easy! How do you convert not liking someone's attitude to an objective fact?

Strangely enough, it comes down to your use of SMART goals.

I say *strangely* for two reasons. First, for us creative and outgoing types, sitting down and writing out goals can seem mundane and daunting.

Second, because SMART goals have been around for decades, a lot of people know about them, but many (or most) don't use them effectively or often enough.

The first known uses of the term *SMART goals* occurred in the November, 1981, issue of *Management Review* by George T. Doran. SMART goals are a way to evaluate the objectives or goals for an individual project. The term is also in common usage in performance management, whereby goals and targets set for employees must fulfill the criteria.

Here's the power of SMART goals: if all the feedback you gave and all your performance appraisals were based on SMART goals, you would avoid being subjective.

Clearly, it's ideal never to have subjective thoughts. Using SMART goals can greatly diminish reliance on subjective thoughts and increase objectivity.

Traditionally taught, SMART stands for:

S   Specific
M   Measurable
A   Attainable
R   Relevant or realistic
T   Timely or trackable

But I believe it can be made simpler.

There are two common reasons why people don't create SMART goals:

- They don't have the time.
- It can get too complex.

They don't have the time

The concept of time is an issue that both managers and non-managers have to deal with on a daily basis. Time management is for everyone but the time spent on great SMART goals saves you a lot of time after you have created them. It can potentially save you thousands of hours and thousands of dollars. It's worth doing!

You also don't have to do them all. You can delegate creating SMART goals to your employees so they will understand, gain responsibility and take ownership for the goals they need to attain.

It can get too complex

Creating SMART goals can get too complex. Therefore, I've created a tiered approach which simplifies it and (hopefully) increases the chances you will create SMART goals.

SMART goals revised

Tier 1

Focus on the S, M and T portion only. Why? S, M and T are objective, A and R are subjective.

If every action an employee or a manager takes can be categorized by a goal that is specific, measurable and timely, then you can review actions against goals when giving feedback, and when evaluating progress and performance.

So in tier 1 the SMART goal becomes an SMT goal.

Tier 2

After doing S, M and T, then do A and R. However, change the A from *attainable* to *analysis* and the R from *relevant* or *realistic* to *reason*.

When you make *A for analysis* you can look at all the possible ways you won't not meet the goal. This can help you when putting together discussions, and getting resources to help.

In the Time Management workshop I teach at AMA (American Management Association), we teach the analysis as an identifier of roadblocks so you can anticipate the obstacles - the things that could get in the way.

For example, financial issues that might block the goal from being achieved, or political issues such as upper management opposition to the idea, can halt the outcome of a goal.

R for reason aligns with Tony Robbins' process for creating goals. If you remember the reason you are pursuing the goal, you are re-connecting with the motivation to get it done. This is helpful when you get caught up with other things going on in life. Motivation when remembered helps you move forward toward goals you might not look at otherwise.

Tier 1 is SMT (which are all objective measurements) and tier 2 is SMTAR (where the A and R is subjective). Tier 2 can provide more in depth information but tier 1 is enough to create a goal which will help solidify objectivity. You can't create a tier 2 goal without creating a tier 1 goal. Therefore we will practice writing SMT goals.

In the real world, priorities change as the year progresses. But when you have three distinct characteristics of a goal (specific, measurable and timely) you can change one of them if you need to.

Creating SMT goals

Creating SMT goals takes practice. The more you do it, the better you will get. First, you should practice your own goals. This will make it easier to write goals for others.

Here are some initial goals managers have had:

- I want to have a better relationships with my employees.
- I want to improve my communication.
- I want more time to spend on important but not urgent projects.

When you examine each of the above goals you can see how they can only lead to frustrating results. There is nothing specific, measurable or trackable about them! Your evaluation of each of these goals will be based on how you feel about your accomplishments, instead of any specific, measurable and timely standards.

Let's take each of these goals one at a time.

I want to have a better relationship with my employees

Another common trap is grouping all your employees together. Each of your employees is an individual. With which ones specifically would you want better relationships? You need a separate goal for each of them. Furthermore, what does it mean to have "better relationships?"

You can see how you need to ask yourself questions to break down a goal into three distinct parts! If this proves frustrating to do alone, talking with someone else helps immensely.

A broader SMT goal for all employees would be

To know each one of my employees and their strengths

This goal, although not S, M and T, is a step in the right direction. It is more specific (each employee and their strengths) but there is no measurement or time associated with it.

Another variation would be:

Meet with each of my employees weekly for the next two quarters.

While this goal doesn't state what you are meeting about, nor does it measure the effectiveness of the meetings, it is specific (meet with each of my employees), measureable (weekly) and timely (for the next two quarters).

Other SMT goals could be created based on the above goal. Some possibilities:

Have an agenda that we complete at every meeting.

This goal is specific (agenda), measureable (we get through), and timely (every meeting)

You can go even further with the original goal.

Meet weekly with each employee to discuss the five categories of performance for which they are responsible. Complete a form at the end of each meeting which will outline further actions for both the employee and me.

The specific component is *discuss the five categories of performance.* The measureable component is *completion of report.* The time component is *weekly.*

You can see how this could never end! You can always make something more specific or measureable. When do you stop?

When it is working.

It is impossible to have everything covered. The goal is to first look at where your issues lie – start by changing those issues to SMT goals.

I want to be a better communicator

Communication can always be improved, so it would be beneficial to make this goal be more specific, measurable, and timely.

With whom do you want to improve your communication? How will you know if your communication is improved? Or do you really feel it can be improved with everyone from your employees to your peers to your boss? What can be improved? Are you not getting the results you want?

If this is a broad goal you can keep it that way and still make it an SMT goal.

For example: *take a communications workshop within the next three months and learn at least two specific tools I can use to communicate with others.*

While you definitely can get more specific, this goal meets all three standards (SMT) and has significantly more direction than the original goal written.

I want more time to spend on important but not urgent projects.

This goal was created by a manager attending one of my workshops. It makes sense because she learned there were several things she could do to be a more effective manager (such as taking the time to meet regularly with her employees, creating goals for herself and her employees, delegating to them, and taking the time to do it efficiently).

So her intent was in the right place. But without setting a timeframe and a measurable objective, her sense of success or failure will be based on mood and subjectivity. Just shifting this goal a little bit to come up with specific, measurable and timely actions will make it more objective.

For example: *spend 15 minutes twice a day doing important but not urgent work.*

The specific is *important but not urgent work*; the measurable is *15 minutes*; the timely is *twice a day*.

By having this measurement, this manager can see if this time allotment is working for her or adjust the goal until she meets it. She could adjust the measurable time of 15 minutes or the frequency of twice a day to what will suit her best.

In summary, the more your goals align towards SMT (specific, measureable, timely):

- The greater chance you have to be objective since you have something to measure an employee against.
- The more effective a coach you'll be because you have a framework of what is going well or what isn't going well. This gives you a basis for a discussion.
- Your focus can be targeted to objective facts rather than your subjective opinions.
- It will help you in giving both positive and constructive feedback.
- The projects you delegate will have a greater chance for success since the outcome is more defined.

Tool 2: Examining behavior

We all react and behave differently. This isn't right or wrong, it simply is.

But since we don't appreciate or remember that other people respond differently. Therefore we succumb to us being right and them being wrong, thinking subjectively and forgetting to focus on the facts.

So a solution is to identify someone else's behavior and do actions based on the answers to your questions.

What's written here is based on the DiSC* behavioral assessment tool which has been around since the 1920's. More detail on the history of the DiSC can be found in the resource section of this book.

In general, there are four styles of behaviors. We all have the ability to use all four styles, but one or two are usually more dominant to us than the other ones. These dominant behaviors may not be someone else's dominant behaviors.

These four styles encompass two different traits.

- People are generally either fast-paced or moderate-paced*
- People are also either people-oriented or task-oriented.

*You should realize anyone who is fast paced would want to call the others slow-paced – but since slow comes from a judgment, its better not to call them slow paced, but moderate- paced.

To examine someone's behavior in a situation so you move from subjectivity to objectivity you only need to ask yourself two questions:

- *Is this person fast-paced or moderate-paced?*
- *Is this person task-oriented or people-oriented?*

The objective is to match your actions with their style.

For example, if you are moderate paced, but dealing with someone who is fast-paced and wants results, you give them choices and stick to the bottom line.

If you're fast-paced and dealing with someone who likes all the details (moderate pace and task oriented), take the time to document what you were talking about and present it to them so they can analyze the information.

What you're doing is giving someone what they need in order to help them communicate. More effective communications leads to objectivity.

The table in the resource section of this book gives you insight on how someone with those characteristics likes to be approached. For example, the fast paced/task oriented person wants you to be direct with them while offering choices, while the moderate paced/people oriented person needs re-assurance and sincere appreciation.

When you ask yourself the two questions (*Is this person fast-paced or moderate-paced* and *is this person task-oriented or people-oriented*) and you don't know the answer, make the assumption they are people-oriented and moderate paced.

It might surprise you to know almost 50% of people are people oriented and moderate paced (this will surprise all the fast-paced people out there!)

Tool 3: Five parts to a complete message

This tool is based on examples from Emotional Intelligence. Emotional Intelligence is a relatively new concept, developed in the 1990's, which examines how intelligently/effectively you handle your emotions in a professional environment. Research has found that the more constructive your emotions, the greater chance for promotion.

This tool is something you can use either in person or in writing. It helps you deliver a complete message to minimize miscommunication.

The first advantage of using this tool is that it gets you to stop, pause, reflect and think about what you want to say. This is especially helpful when you are feeling angry or frustrated.

The five parts to a complete message are:

- Fact – every message needs a fact.
- Opinion – every message needs an opinion you want to express.
- Feeling – every message should express your feelings
- Need – this expresses what you need.
- Conclusion – either a question or statement which wraps up the complete message.

Your message doesn't have to be in this order but it must have one of each: one fact, one opinion, one feeling, one need and one conclusion.

This doesn't all have to be one sentence; there could be many sentences which incorporate the complete message.

Let's review each part in more detail.

Fact: this is the hardest part. Many of us think our opinions are facts. This is especially true when we are in conflict. The idea is to have a fact that can't be argued. As a general rule, the shorter the sentence the more likely it is a fact! Of course it is possible a long sentence is a fact, but messages often contain facts buried under an opinion. For example, the statement *I was listening to your call and it sounded like you could use more excitement* is not a fact. But saying *I was listening to your call* is a fact (whether you were effectively listening or not doesn't matter for this particular fact).

Ideally, the *fact* should have a characteristic from an SMT goal (something specific, measurable or timely).

Opinion: this is the easiest part! Often we give opinion after opinion. Our opinions are important but only one opinion per message.

Feeling: why do we need to include how we feel about what's going on? Two reasons: to show we are involved and to let the other person know what they do has an effect on others. The feeling statement should never begin with *"you"* (for example, you made me angry) but rather with an *"I"* statement (I am angry).

People can be uncomfortable expressing their feelings. The following are feelings which may not be as intimidating to use:

- Annoyed
- Appreciated
- Concerned
- Confused
- Frustrated
- Glad
- Grateful
- Impressed
- Irritated
- Pleased
- Proud
- Relieved
- Satisfied
- Surprised
- Uncomfortable

Need: if you don't know what you need, then why are you having the conversation?! Sometimes coming up with the need statement takes the hardest thinking on your part. When you state a need there should always be these two words in the statement: *I need*. Not *I would really like you to* or *I would prefer if* or *I really want you* – but *I need*!

Conclusion – after you have stated or written one fact, one opinion, one feeling and one need, you conclude the message with either a statement or a question.

The tone of all these parts will depend on who you are speaking to. This complete message tool can be used with your employees, your manager or upper management, or your peers. What you need might be said differently depending on who the message is for.

Further detail on *fact*:

Of the following which one is <u>not</u> an obvious fact?

1. The two tests were to be completed on Aug 27 for internal review and I haven't seen them yet.
2. I have not received the two test plans you are required to prepare for the simulation project.
3. The deadline for the two test plans has passed and I don't have them yet.

The answer is #2. The reason is not a fact is because *you are required to prepare* could be debated. If this is spelled out in a performance measurement then it could be a fact. But it could also be an opinion; perhaps this person thinks someone else is required to prepare the project.

The aim in stating (or writing) a *fact* is to have it *non debatable*.

When you are struggling to write a fact, an alternative is to present a fact that isn't directly related to what you need.

For example, consider the following scenario:

You have an employee whose overall performance has slipped on multiple projects. She seems to always have reasons why things haven't been completed to standard or on time. No progress has been made despite repeated talks with her.

While you would want to have continuous feedback sessions with your employee, and also come up with a motivating reward or consequence, start with a five part complete statement.

This scenario came from a manager in one of my workshops. When this scenario was given to the class to write up as a complete message, they struggled with the <u>fact</u>. Every fact they wrote (*you were late on project A, project B was missing information,* and so on) would be argued by the employee; this is what the manager who presented the scenario told us!

So the trick is to come up with a fact that isn't directly related.

For example: *You have been with this company for six years.*

This fact couldn't be argued. While it's not directly related to the problem or what you need to address, you can use the fact as follows:

You have with this company for six years. Your performance has been below par. I'm concerned because if it doesn't improve you might lose your job. I need several things turned around. How can we work together to accomplish this goal?

Dissecting the above situation:

Fact: You have with this company for six years.

Opinion: Your performance has been below par.

Feeling: I'm concerned because if it doesn't improve you might lose your job.

Need: I need several things turned around.

Conclusion: How can we work together to accomplish this goal?

For further examples of complete messages, see the appendix section of this book.

Tool 4: How to increase listening

- Get conscious about listening more and talking less.
- Turn away from your computer and blackberry/iPhone while talking to someone.
- Come up with a time – 90 seconds to two minutes – where you consciously decide to let someone talk without interrupting.
- If you have trouble keeping quiet, putting a finger over your mouth can get you to remember to wait a bit before you speak!
- Remember that *listening is your job.*

Tool 5: Asking questions that lead to solutions

Listed are some questions which lead to solutions - there are an infinite number! They are in four different categories, although you might find some questions go into more than one category.

Depending on the situation, a question might lead to opportunity or not. The only way you know is to try it – if the answers lead to alternatives then it's an opportunity; if the answers lead to more headache and impossibilities, *it's not a good question, try another!*

Talking to a employee with poor performance

1. In your current job, what are you favorite things to do?
2. In your current job, what could be better?
3. How can I best support you?
4. How do you measure your success?
5. Which areas do you think need improvement?
6. What's one thing you can do to raise your performance level?
7. What's working for you?
8. What's not working for you?
9. What daily habits or routines do you want to create?
10. What daily habits or routines would you like to stop?

Project behind schedule

1. What prevented the project from being done on time?
2. How can we correct it?
3. What can I do to help?
4. What needs to be done to move the project along?
5. What's one thing we can do right now?
6. How do we avoid any more delay?
7. What support do you need?
8. Who else should we involve?
9. What can we do differently?
10. What are your top priorities?

Career development/growth

1. What activities excite you?
2. What other jobs do you see yourself having?
3. What aspects of your current job do you love?
4. If you didn't have to work, what would you do?
5. What motivates you?
6. Who do you admire and why?
7. What else would you like to learn?
8. What opportunities are out there for you?
9. What do you enjoy doing?
10. What advice would you give someone who has your current job?

General Questions

1. What else?
2. What's next?
3. How else can I see the situation?
4. Is what I'm saying entirely true?
5. What is great about this situation/problem?
6. What is not perfect yet?
7. What am I willing to do to make it the way I want it?
8. What's wrong?
9. What would you like to change?
10. What if it doesn't always have to be this way?

Howard Miller

Appendix

Behavior Examples

Review the two questions to ask to figure out someone's behavioral style:

- *Is this person is fast-paced or moderate-paced?*
- *Is this person task-oriented or people-oriented?*

Scenario #1

Fred is the manager and is fast-paced and task-oriented. He is constantly frustrated with his employee Diane because she is continually late with getting her projects done.

Up until now he kept confronting her by asking what is preventing her from meeting the deadline. He wasn't getting any satisfactory answers. So while this is a good question at times, in this case it's not a good question because no solution or alternative actions are being discussed.

Fred decides to examine Diane's behavior. He sees that she is resistant to change and has difficulty prioritizing. When asking the two questions above, he realizes that she is moderate paced, people oriented, while he is fast paced and task oriented.

Using the chart on Page 109, what are two things Fred can do differently?

Some possible answers include:

- Be a little more patient in explaining what needs to be done.
- If possible, warn Diane of changes in advance.

Scenario #2

Danny is frustrated with his employee Sylvia. While she is enthusiastic, she is also unorganized and doesn't provide the specifics Danny needs and desires. Her email responses to Danny's questions are vague. It seems like she is doing the work, but she does not provide detailed information about what she is doing.

Since the email exchanges and meetings don't seem to provide any results, Danny decided to examine his and her behavior. After asking the two questions, he sees that he is moderate-paced and task-oriented while Sylvia is fast-paced and people-oriented.

Using the chart below (Changing the pace at which you react) what are two things Danny can do differently?

Some possible answers include:

- Engage Sylvia in conversation and let the talking lead to the detailed information he is seeking. Conversely, if Sylvia were trying to change her behavior, she would want to put more details into writing because she would realize this interaction works better for Danny.
- Explain to Sylvia how this work is important and put Sylvia in the limelight.

Scenario #3

Carla wants results and her employee Susan takes forever to get them. She builds rapport well and has great relationships, but she takes longer to produce results than any other member of the team. When Carla asks Susan when she'll get the results, she hears a long explanation of what's going on but she doesn't get the results she seeks.

Carla decides to try a new approach and look at how Susan behaves. She knows she is fast-paced and task-oriented. She feels Susan is also fast-paced but definitely people-oriented.

What can Carla do differently to help and change the way they interact so they can get better results?

Some possible answers include:

- Let Susan talk and verbalize her thoughts, then ask her to commit to some actions.
- Show Susan how important it is for her to follow through.

Putting the result of this conversation in writing benefits both the manager and the employee.

Changing the Pace at Which You React

If the other person is fast-paced and task-oriented, try to:	If the other person is fast-paced and people-oriented, try to:
• make communication brief and to the point • respect her need for autonomy • be clear about rules and expectations	• approach him informally • be relaxed and sociable • let him verbalize thoughts and feelings
To meet their needs: • be factual • be direct • offer choices	To meet their needs: • be flexible • acknowledge him • help him follow through
Be prepared for: • blunt, demanding approaches • lack of empathy • little social interaction	Be prepared for: • attempts to persuade or influence others • need for the limelight • overestimation of self and others

Howard Miller

If the other person Is moderate-paced and task-oriented, try to:	If the other person is moderate-paced and people-oriented, try to:
• give clear expectations and deadlines • demonstrate loyalty • be tactful and emotionally reserved	• use sincere appreciation • show their importance to the organization • let her adapt slowly to change
To meet their needs: • be logical • be thorough • support your facts with data	To meet their needs: • be sincere • accept and appreciate her • warn her of changes in advance
Be prepared for: • discomfort with ambiguity • resistance to vague or general information • desire to double-check	Be prepared for: • friendliness to colleagues and supervisors • resistance to change • difficulty identifying priorities and deadlines

DISC Behavioral Profile: A Brief Background

Throughout the ages, Man has been trying to explain the behavior of his counterparts. Back in 444 B.C., Empedocles believed that people would behave in a certain way when they got into contact with different elements like Earth, Air, Fire or Water. Hippocrates, however, believed that it is the type of fluids that flowed in a person that determines how he or she will behave - cold or warm, fast or slow moving fluids - give rise to different personality types: Choleric, Sanguine, Phlegmatic and Melancholic. In 1921, Carl Gustav Jung introduced four different psychological types of personality: Thinking, Feeling, Sensation and Intuition that influences a person's behavior.

Finally in 1926, William M. Marston (also the inventor of the lie detector test and creator of the comic character Wonder Woman!) invented the Dominance, Influence, Steadiness and Compliance (D.I.S.C.) personality system, which has benefited many individuals and organizations in better understanding their most valuable asset –people.

The four aspects of behavior identified by Dr. Marston are:

- Dominance – being results oriented, direct and decisive.
- Influence – being interactive, influencing and sociable.
- Steadiness – being stable, steady and secure.
- Compliance - being compliant, correct and controlled.

Understanding behavior styles can and has helped many organizations, both large and small, in many of the following areas:

- Team building
- Motivation
- Communication
- Conflict Resolution/Prevention
- Increasing Retention and Morale
- Job Placement

Examples of complete messages

Scenario: Your employee seems to leave work early often.

Possible complete message (there are countless options!):

Fact: You left work at 5PM today. (The *trap* would be to reference being late more then once. Focus on this one time in order to make the fact more specific and less confrontational or argumentative.)

Opinion: I had some work I needed you to finish up. (This might seem like a fact, but it's what you wanted, not a given)

Feeling: I'm concerned because this isn't the first time this has happened (This is bordering on an opinion, but the "concern" makes it a feeling)

Need: I need you to do the work I assign you.

Conclusion: What will get in the way of accomplishing this? (This question invites a discussion)

Scenario: Your employee is late delivering work on a project.

Possible complete message (there are countless options!):

Fact: The deadline for the two test plans was yesterday. (The trap managers fall into is to say "you missed the deadline." Then the focus shifts to why the employee is late delivering, as opposed to focusing on completing the work.)

Opinion: Test plan delivery is vital for the end success of the project.

Feeling: I'm concerned because these plans are late.

Need: I need the plans as soon as possible.

Conclusion: When can you get them to me?

Scenario: Your employee is consistently late with a report. Despite numerous conversations, this hasn't changed. Further, he has an excuse every time he's late.

Possible complete message (there are countless options!):

Fact: You are a full time employee. (The trap could be to mention any of the times the employee is late since he is so argumentative. So this is one of those times when using an unrelated fact could be better.)

Opinion: One of your roles is to complete an accurate cycle report by 8AM every day.

Feeling: I'm frustrated because despite our numerous conversations, this isn't happening.

Need: I need you to complete daily reports on time, otherwise you will have a lower performance evaluation. (If it is true that you can and will give a lower performance evaluation, it is appropriate to tie this consequence with the need.)

Conclusion: I hope this is clear. (In this case, ending with a statement would be stronger then a question since this isn't up for discussion.)

Scenario: Your employee has a reputation for being moody and negative in meetings. You have heard this from others and have seen it yourself.

Fact: In the meeting this morning, you mentioned the negative consequences of working using the ABC method. (The *trap* managers can fall into is to say that the employee comes across as negative. Though shared by many, this is an opinion and not a fact. Be as specific as you can.)

Opinion: While it's part of our job to mention negative consequences, I think it's also important to mention what could go right.

Feeling: I'm frustrated because I don't think you're being shown in the best light. (This feeling ties right into your opinion, which is a natural follow-on from the fact).

Need: I need you to say something that goes right every time you mention something that goes wrong. (This need has a specific goal.)

Conclusion: What can we do to facilitate this? (You can guide your employee to the specific goal mentioned in your need, and brainstorm a way for your employee to do this, no matter how ridiculous he thinks it is. You might need to relay a consequence if he doesn't align a positive statement with a negative statement, but this is a good start to getting him to do what you need.)

Scenario: An employee always seems angry.

Fact: Yesterday you came into my office.

Opinion: It seemed to me you were angry.

Feeling: I'm frustrated because I can't help you.

Need: I need you to let me know how I can help you.

Conclusion: What can we both do to facilitate this?

(This situation is a difficult one. It could be that no matter what you say, you won't get a response or you will elicit more perceived anger or silence. The response written above is not confrontational but it is direct. It shows you are willing to help and not matching anger with anger.)

It takes practice to implement the five parts to a complete message effectively. But with practice, you will be able to quickly combine effective facts, opinions, feelings, needs and a conclusion. This will help reduce the likelihood of falling into common manager pitfalls.

Workbook Section

This section contains questions for you to answer to help you get into action based on the traps, pitfalls and tools mentioned in this book.

Think of an employee with whom you are having issues.

What are the issues?

_____

_____

_____

_____

_____

_____

_____

_____

_____

_____

_____

_____

_____

_____

_____

_____

_____

_____

_____

_____

_____

_____

_____

Now, read what you wrote.

How much of it is objective and how much is subjective?

_____
_____
_____
_____
_____
_____
_____

Change the subjective to objective.

_____
_____
_____
_____
_____
_____
_____
_____
_____
_____
_____
_____
_____
_____
_____
_____
_____
_____

_____

_____

_____

_____

_____

_____

_____

_____

_____

_____

_____

_____

_____

_____

List the items are you having trouble changing from subjective to objective.

_____

_____

_____

_____

_____

_____

_____

_____

_____

_____

_____

_____

For everything objective: is it specific, measureable and timely? (SMT)

_____
_____
_____
_____
_____
_____
_____
_____
_____
_____
_____
_____
_____
_____
_____
_____
_____
_____
_____
_____
_____
_____
_____
_____

Have you communicated these objectives to your employee? How?
How often?

_____

_____

_____

_____

_____

_____

_____

_____

_____

_____

_____

_____

_____

_____

_____

_____

_____

_____

_____

_____

_____

_____

_____

What can you do differently?

_____

_____

_____

_____

_____

_____

_____

_____

_____

_____

_____

_____

_____

_____

_____

_____

_____

_____

_____

_____

_____

_____

_____

_____

Howard Miller

Are you using the five parts to a complete message? If so, write one here:

_____

_____

_____

_____

_____

_____

_____

_____

_____

_____

_____

_____

_____

_____

_____

_____

_____

_____

_____

_____

_____

_____

_____

_____

_____

_____

_____

_____

_____

_____

_____

_____

_____

Is the employee fast paced or moderate paced?

_____
_____
_____
_____

Is the employee people oriented or task oriented?

_____
_____
_____
_____
_____
_____

Based on these two behavioral characteristics, what actions could you take that you haven't previously taken?

_____
_____
_____
_____
_____
_____
_____
_____
_____
_____
_____
_____
_____
_____
_____
_____
_____

How often do you meet with your employee? Should you increase or decrease the frequency?

_____
_____
_____
_____
_____
_____
_____
_____
_____

Do you have a structure to your meeting?

_____
_____
_____
_____
_____

Do you use the 5 Fs (factual, focused, frequent, freely, fast) when giving feedback?

_____
_____
_____
_____
_____
_____
_____
_____

In your meetings, what percentage of the time are you talking vs. listening? If you are talking more then 50% how can you talk less and listen more?

_____
_____
_____
_____
_____
_____
_____
_____
_____
_____
_____
_____
_____
_____
_____
_____
_____
_____
_____
_____
_____
_____
_____
_____
_____
_____

Identify 5 questions that will shift the focus of your conversation. Use the samples listed in the resource section or make up some of your own.

_____
_____
_____
_____
_____
_____
_____
_____
_____
_____
_____
_____
_____
_____
_____
_____
_____
_____
_____
_____
_____
_____
_____
_____
_____
_____
_____
_____
_____
_____
_____
_____

For everything you have that is subjective:

What prevents you from making it an objective statement?

_____
_____
_____
_____
_____
_____
_____
_____
_____
_____
_____
_____

Is this something that bothers you? What about it bothers you?

_____
_____
_____
_____
_____
_____
_____
_____
_____
_____
_____
_____

Is there something else you can focus on to get results from your employee?

_____

_____

_____

_____

_____

_____

_____

_____

_____

_____

_____

_____

_____

_____

_____

_____

_____

_____

_____

_____

_____

_____

_____

_____

_____

_____

_____

_____

To help you identify what else you can focus on:

- What do they value?
- What motivates them?

What do they value?

_____

_____

_____

_____

_____

_____

_____

_____

_____

_____

_____

_____

_____

_____

_____

_____

_____

_____

_____

_____

_____

_____

What motivates them?

_____
_____
_____
_____
_____
_____
_____
_____
_____
_____
_____
_____
_____
_____
_____
_____
_____
_____
_____
_____
_____
_____
_____
_____
_____

So, what should you focus on to get results from your employees?

_____

_____

_____

_____

_____

_____

_____

_____

_____

_____

_____

_____

_____

_____

_____

_____

_____

_____

_____

_____

_____

_____

_____

_____

_____

_____

_____

_____

_____

_____

_____

_____

_____

Howard Miller

Soundbites

Prior to this book, I wrote *You're Full of Shift*, a collection of real life situations where my clients or I shifted difficult situations to opportunities.

These soundbites continue to this day, but they are now focused on traps and pitfalls that managers deal with on a daily basis.

Below are a few of those management soundbites, written in a more colloquial style than the rest of this book.

Do you sometimes think things are not fair?

My sister-in-law promised my eldest niece two desserts, one at the restaurant where we were having dinner and then at an ice cream shop. Because dinner took so long, my 7 year old niece was informed there would be no time to go get the ice cream.

But that isn't fair was her response!

After some whining, crying, drama (from her, not me!) and follow up coaching from me and from her 5 year old sister, the issue was resolved. She got the ice cream.

But before the resolution, everything went awry because fairness was not perceived favorably by my niece.

Fairness, or being fair to others, is highly valued by most people.

The Academy of Management lists *fairness* as one of their 54 work values. Whenever I facilitate groups of managers on a values exercise, *fairness* <u>always</u> (and I mean every time, so if I've done 100 facilitations doing this exercise, this has happened 100 times) is in the top 5 of the collected group's values.

I have coached upper managers and executives who aspire to be *fair* to everyone. I have seen white papers written where one of the goals is to be *fair*.

*As a leader or manager do you aspire to be **fair**?*

If you do, stop!

You are setting yourself up for stress, conflict, miscommunication and unproductive time.

Going for fair is a trap. This is because what's fair to you is not necessarily fair to someone else. Fair is a feeling based on our values, experiences and past history. It's not about being right or wrong, and yet if something seems unfair we feel we are being wronged and we're in the right.

Fair is subjective. Subjective measurements and suggestions cannot lead to agreement unless everyone involved sees whatever is happening the exact same way. And the likelihood of this happening in a work environment is as high a probability as a 7 year old accepting she can't have her ice cream because the service in a restaurant was too slow!

As we start to recognize the trap of using the word fair:

- We can recognize how much or little we each use the word.
- We will see how much the word is used by others.
- We can start to focus on how to use objective measurements instead of the subjective *fair*.

And when you start to do this, ironically you will be heading towards being fair!

You didn't say I'd be fired!

One of my clients told me of a time where he had a problem employee. He increased his feedback to his employee, telling him if he didn't shape up, he'd be let go. The employee never improved.

So one day, this manager called the employee into the room to tell him he was fired. The employee was shocked.

The manager was confused. He said to his employee *"I told you if you didn't shape up you'd be let go."*

The employee's response: *"Yes, but you didn't say I'd be fired."*

This employee was a blithering idiot, right? Well, maybe not.

What else could *let go* mean?

It could mean transferred to a different department, different manager, and different position.

Maybe the employee thought *I'd be let go to another department* or *I'd be let go to another position*, or *finally - I'll be let go and away from this manager I can't stand!*

Whether it was denial, ignorance, hearing what we want to hear – we all have been on the employee side of this. I know I have – with peers, friends and family. Especially family!

And as managers, our best attempts to be clear can still lead to different conclusions then what we were intending.

Are there any fool-proof ways of getting communication right?

Well, no.

But there are steps you can take to minimize miscommunication. They can include making sure you understand what you are comfortable saying and not saying, getting your employee (or the person you're communicating to) to repeat back what she heard, and following up if the issue is one that will continue over a period of time.

When I accept that my best and obvious communications can still be received in a way I didn't attend:

- I try to be more specific in precarious situations.
- I listen and observe more after the conversation to see if anything has changed.
- I stop before I talk to think (and even write) things through.

The brilliance of communications is that it can involve so much interpretation and creativity. And therein lays the challenge as well.

Always isn't every time

As a manager, do you and your employees have miscommunication?

How do you interpret it when someone says they always do something?

I do an exercise in my management skills workshops to demonstrate how easy it is to misinterpret communications.

I have everyone write down common words we all use, such as *frequently, occasionally, never* and *always.*

I then have them put a number next to each word, from 0 to 100. The number represents the percentage they feel the word means.

Naturally, there are a lot of numbers and ranges for words such as *frequently* and *occasionally.*

But when I first did this exercise, I wrote 100% for *always* and 0% for *never.*

My logic told me if someone says *always* it means all the time, therefore 100%. And if someone says *never* they mean not at all, which interprets to 0%.

I was initially surprised when people did not share my logic. Now I know people will not share my logic.

I have done this exercise several hundred times.

I have NEVER had every single person pick 100% for *always* or 0% for *never.*

And I mean that literally!

People's interpretations of these words have to do with their experiences such as broken promises from others. People with such a history don't take what others say at face value.

This shows me is how easy it is to have miscommunication. If we misinterpret the so-called easy words, how do we manage the more complex ones?!

When I realize how easy it is to misinterpret what is said:

- I try to talk in specifics.
- I have the other person repeat back what was said even if it seems obvious.
- I ask the other person to clarify what they are saying; more often if I don't understand, or if I think it could lead to misinterpretation.

Miscommunication leads to lack of understanding which leads to frustration. Clearing it up takes time, but it may only take seconds and save hours of frustration!

Not always, but sometimes!

Just the facts

Do any of your employees (or does anyone at all) continually challenge you in an unproductive way?

More than likely it's because you are letting your emotions, instead of the actual facts, guide your leadership.

As human beings, emotions are part of us and vital to living life to their fullest. But emotions easily get in the way of effective decision making, whether we are managers, entrepreneurs, or employees.

They get us into difficult situations, which can lead to open conflicts with some people, avoidance of others, and rising blood pressure within ourselves.

The trick is to convert any emotional issue into a measurable fact.

For example, a manager in a recent workshop was frustrated by a moody employee. This manager felt the employee's moodiness was a downer and affected morale.

Okay, but how would you approach the employee? If you tell him that he is moody, he may react by becoming argumentative, denying the accusation, or filing charges for harassment.

If you can convert moodiness to a fact, you have a measurable way in.

For example, you could say: *In last week's meeting, you predicted this project would go wrong.*

You can use this fact you to create a conversation about the difficulty of saying things like this, and you can suggest that your employee balance statements about how the project could go wrong with statements about how it could succeed.

Either way you're avoiding the word *moody*. You are using facts.

If you can't find a fact, it means the issue is personal to you and it probably does not need to be resolved for the greater good. If this is the case, accepting it and leaving it as is will alleviate potentially irresolvable conflict.

When you use facts to present situations which need to be resolved:

- Make sure you have thought about the situation before talking about it.
- Shift the focus of conversation to something that can be managed.
- Recognize the issue isn't about you and your values.

Shifting feelings into facts gets easier the more you do it.

And it *feels* good!

Do you ever commit to things that you possibly can't achieve?

"My door is always open."

In his nationally televised State of the Union address, President Barack Obama said he wanted to hear all ideas. He said *"My door is always open."*

Really?

So if I just happened to go to Washington DC and went to the White House, I would immediately be admitted to the oval office to talk with the president?

Okay, that's ridiculous, I'm an ordinary citizen.

Did he mean a senator or congressman who wanted to talk to him could just walk in?

Doubtful, Very doubtful.

The senator or congressman could see the president but only by making an appointment since his schedule is pretty busy.

Well, your schedule is pretty busy too.

Do you ever use that blanket statement *my door is always open*? Do you ever hear anyone else say it?

It's a standard that you can't possibly meet.

Now you might ask, what's the harm, it's only a statement, everyone uses it and no one means it literally.

But this kind of thinking sets you up. It gets you to not keep your word. Not keeping our word leads to miscommunication. Miscommunication is one of the biggest challenges of all managers, leaders and entrepreneurs.

When dealing with employees who need your guidance, it would be more meaningful to say something like *"If you have any questions, email me anytime."* This gives an avenue of support without committing to a particular response time. (Unless you tell them you'll respond right away, but that's another issue!)

When we realize what we say matters and stop using reflexive colloquialisms:

- People will start to take what we say more literally.
- We help facilitate a clear direction for getting things done.
- We stand apart from most managers, leaders and entrepreneurs.

Do you have an employee who takes advantage of the system?

My employee seems to be sick on Fridays and Mondays.

In a recent tennis match, one of my teammates was angry after his match. He lost and felt the other team didn't really play good tennis. He said *all they did was lob the ball, and it wasn't fun*. But it was a legal strategy and it worked.

Similarly, having an employee who seems to be sick right before or after a weekend could be very frustrating. It leads to all sorts of conclusions, doesn't it?

Let's face I, we don't think they're sick, do we?

So, what can you do about it? If your company has an attendance policy and the employee is complying with it, there really is nothing you can do to stop it.

But that's not fair. It doesn't set a good example to the rest of the team.

But it's legal. If the company has set policy and the employee is following it, you need to live by the policy unless you are in a position to change it.

But I don't trust them. They are getting away with something and I don't like it.

Ah, the challenges of being a manager or business owner with employees!

So what can you do?

Change your question to change your focus

Your focus is completely subjective and attempting to come up with solutions based on your subjectivity will lead to increased frustration and no results.

So objectively – what's the issue with the employee being out? Are they doing their work?

If the answer is *yes, but they could be doing more,* you need to define the "more."

If the answer is *yes, but it's not fair,* then what you need to do is let go – this is your issue, causing you frustration, anger, stress or whatever unpleasantness you're experiencing. I know this is easier said then done; one of the biggest challenges for managers is to put their personal values aside.

If the answer is no, what aren't they doing? Focus on that – if it's a measurable goal already in writing, use that for reference. If its not, get it in writing and get it in their performance plan!

When you have frustrating situations and you ask yourself questions that shift your focus:

- You can shift from an issue with no answers to something with an objective measurement.
- You can let go of personal frustration.
- You can focus on results.

That person has a difficult personality

Does it irritate you when one of your employees, peers, or boss is very difficult?

They just have that personality which gets under your skin. They seem to always be negative and never smile. Or they seem to always be optimistic and not realistic. Or some other irritating attribute.

Getting irritated by someone's personality is an opportunity to change the relationship! What you need to do is look at it differently.

When I teach skills to managers I don't allow them to use the word *personality*. I have them use the word *behavior*. If they slip and use *personality* I have them change it to *behavior* (well, by the second day, they're making the change themselves!)

Why this focus? What's the difference between using the word *behavior* or *personality*?

Unless we are a psychiatrist who can prescribe mind altering drugs or we are one of those characters with supernatural powers on the now defunct television show *Heroes*, we don't have the power to change someone's personality. It is a trap and pitfall to focus on changing their *personality* or even be bothered by it. It increases one's stress level and doesn't lead to anything productive.

What we can change is our *behavior*. Not *their* behavior. But *our* behavior.

For example, if we feel we're always talking to someone and they never seem to do what we want, maybe we should stop talking! They might prefer email.

Or if we deal with someone who seems always in a rush and is intimidating, maybe we should behave like they do. When we approach them, we can be brief and to the point, and offer solutions in our conversation.

When we focus on how someone behaves instead of her personality:

- We put responsibility on ourselves.
- We can take action to change the situation.
- We can change our behavior to match or complement theirs.

Changing our behavior does not guarantee that someone won't still be difficult. But not changing our behavior pretty much ensures that things will stay the same.

Gen X, Gen Y, Gen whatever

Do you have opinions on someone based on their age?

An attendee in a management workshop I was facilitating was having issues dealing with all the young, twenty-something employees (is this Gen Y?). He sensed they felt entitled and didn't work hard enough.

Another attendee was younger and was intimidated managing people old enough to be her parents.

A third student wanted my opinion about whether managers should focus on generational issues.

I enjoyed that question. I had a simple answer: No!

Now, I know there are books written on how to deal with the different generations, but in my opinion is that looking at this as an issue creates a *focus vacuum*. Focusing on this gets you no where, leads to no solution, yet builds your frustration. *It's a trap.*

While there is truth to some of the generalities associated with each generation, they are just generalities.

Did the attendee who felt twenty-somethings didn't work hard enough see the irony that another attendee in her 20's was struggling dealing with older employees?!

There are twenty-something's who fit the generalities. But also, there are people in their thirties, forties and beyond who fit the generalities ascribed to twenty-somethings. And there are people in their twenties that fit the generalities of other age groups.

If you take the focus off generalities of an age group and look at each person:

- You can measure each person based on their objective goals.
- You will see people of all ages have strengths and challenges.
- You de-emphasize age and emphasize other traits.

However, fifty is definitely the new thirty!

The Facebook Revolution

Do you wonder what your employees are doing on their computer?

Facebook has invaded our lives.

Whether it's connecting with old friends, people we just met, friends of friends, or following opinions about all the hot topics, Facebook is a vehicle to do all of this.

Further, companies have found business reasons to use Facebook for marketing.

You know your staff is in Facebook. But for what reasons? Is it business? Is it personal? How can you control it?

There have been stories of employees who have called in sick – only to update their facebook that day saying they are at the ballgame (I know, what were they thinking?! People don't realize how technology can get them into trouble. This doesn't make sense since technology has been getting a lot of people in trouble for years; anyone remember Oliver North and the Iran-Contra affair?)

But how much focus should you as a manager put into all this?

Focusing on something you can't control can lead you to increased stress, decrease your productivity and get you nowhere.

Everyone does personal things at work – the longer you're at work the more likely you'll need to.

At least using Facebook is quieter than being on the phone.

There have always been inventions which enhance and detract from our productivity. They will always invade our work.

As managers and entrepreneurs with employees - where do we cross the line trying to control this?

If work is getting done, maybe the distraction of reading that an old high school friend had an emergency root canal put an employee in a better mood--because she realized she'd rather be at work then having a root canal! Or if she envies the root canal, perhaps she'll take a serious look at how she is spending countless hours of life!

When you know what is worth your attention:

- You start to own your time rather than feeling others own it.
- Your focus is on solutions.
- You can be more proactive.

And then you too will have time to be on Facebook.

Not listening can be catastrophic

Do you feel your employees are not *listening* to you?!

No matter what you say, or how many times you say it, they don't do what you want?

Obviously, they aren't listening!

But is it easy to listen?

Remember the *telephone game* kid's play? This is where you whisper a phrase or sentence to another player. They then whisper to someone else what they thought they heard. By the time it gets to the last person the message is usually quite different from how it started.

Our communication with employees and peers can be like that as well.

One of the listening exercises I do with managers regarding communications is an adult version of the *telephone game*.

I pretend I'm an executive in a rush – I bump into a manager in the hall, relay some information to them. They need to rely it to someone else. By the end, most pertinent points are missing, names originally talked about are gone, made up people are mentioned and outcomes are completely changed! (What I do is have several volunteers leave the room so they don't know what's going on – they are each called in one by one.)

The last time I did this exercise the first person to follow after me added the word *catastrophic*. I didn't say this word – I said "Certain *measures would have to happen if things didn't change."* They said *"The results would be* **catastrophic** *if things didn't change."*

Through the next iterations of the exercise the message changed quite a bit. What didn't change was the word *catastrophic*. Everyone used it! It remained in each message.

Well, apparently everyone heard the word *catastrophic*!

This makes sense, doesn't it? It's a big word, a dramatic word; its several syllables and fun to say.

But it also proves the point – we only listen to what interests us or what captures our attention.

And what most people say doesn't interest us!

What's important to you to communicate may not be primary for others to hear. While it might be critical, they may not have the focus or urgency to do so at the time you're talking.

Listening takes work.

When we recognize listening is a skill and practice it:

- We allow more two-way conversation as opposed to doing all the talking.
- We try different methods of communication in search of one that makes it easier for others to listen.
- We do our best to have important conversations at a time of day where one can focus on listening.

Listening is powerful. Hearing something differently, even one word incorrectly, can be catastrophic.
Knowing that listening is a skill can help us with the importance of what we say and how we say it.

Dealing with Morons

Do you ever think you're working with people who just don't know what they're doing?!

I was working with a manager who bluntly said most of his wasted time was due to working with a bunch of *morons*.

The *morons* were not his employees, but the clients he and his employees had to service. They were disorganized and always had last minute emergencies. These so-called emergencies cut into what he needed to do during the day, resulting in longer days for him. Most days he worked through lunch and didn't eat.

When he told me this I said: *"You're working through lunch, not eating, and they are the morons?!"*

Don't get me wrong, I'm glad he expressed his frustration exactly the way he did.

Because it showed exactly why he was in this situation.

Calling others *morons* takes the responsibility from you. If others are *morons* you can't change them, therefore you can't change anything about situations where they're involved.

All attempts to change this situation must begin with the same action:

Stop calling others morons!

People might seem to have last minute emergencies all the time, and they might be disorganized, but using these terms to describe the circumstances is very different from being flip and calling them a name.

When you stop using the word *morons* and become specific about actions that cause you frustration:

- You are narrowing your focus to see the issues, one at a time.
- You stop the blame game.
- You start taking responsibility for what you can do to change the situation.

If you and your staff have jobs where a large part of your responsibility is customer service, whether internal or external, you should expect a good chunk of your time will be interrupted by people presenting these issues. Therefore you need to leave time to deal with these unknown actions.

Doing this could be one solution towards working with these *morons*. Then maybe they won't be *morons*.

Having your cake and eating it too

Do you find yourself or others using phrases that you really don't understand?

One of my clients is climbing the management ladder at his company, taking on more responsibility and more ownership.

Looking at how best to deal with employees of all caliber, from the outstanding to the mediocre to the below average, always presents challenges.

While discussing one of his employees, I said "It sounds like *you want to have your cake and eat it too."*

He responded that he never understood this statement. Who wouldn't eat the cake if they had it?!

It made me pause. While I can't remember the exact reason I said this, I do know I was using a common expression which generally means one thing and I didn't consciously think it could mean anything else. (According to Wikipedia, the expression *having your caking and eating it too* is similar to the phrases *you can't have it both ways* and *you can't have the best of both worlds*.)

But the reality is catchphrases don't mean the same thing to everyone. Assuming they do leads to misinterpretation, miscommunication and judgment.

I was fortunate my client communicated (and challenged) me on the expression. It got me to rephrase what I was talking about.

But how many of our employees will not say anything, yet interpret the catch phrase differently from how you intend it? What could be the consequences?

If we think about common phrases before or while we use them:

- We can explain what we mean when we use that phrase.
- We can ask the person we're talking to how they interpret the phrase.
- We might not use the phrase!

Then we can start having our cake and eating it too!

Do you ever want something different from your employees, but aren't sure exactly what?!

If you don't know what you need, why are you talking about it?

I have talked with several frustrated managers. They are irritated and/or aggravated by some of their employees.

This is for a variety of reasons, from a perceived lack of employee motivation to feeling the employee is downright lazy.

But there is a universal issue that arises when it comes time for the manager to talk to the employee. The manager usually has trouble articulating what she needs.

If you don't know what you need, then you shouldn't be talking to your employees about the issue or situation!

If you are giving feedback to someone, especially if it is feedback to help them improve or change, you *must* to be able to express what you *need*.

It *needs* to be easy to understand, and it must not be open to interpretation.

The first two words you must use when you express what you *need*:

I need

Not *I would really like you to* or *I want you to*

But...*I need*

If you aren't certain about what you need, don't begin the conversation until you are certain.

It's okay to need to vent, or to be unsure of what you need. This only means that what you *need* is further understanding. Clearly communicate that understanding is what you *need* when you talk to them.

When we express what we *need* in a way that is easy to understand and not open to interpretation:

- We have thought about an issue before speaking.
- We are taking the time to look at the situation.
- We might get what we need!

Are you sometimes hesitant to ask what something means because you think you should know it already?

Pretending to know the acronyms

Industries have acronyms. Corporations have even more. It's engrained in their cultures.

But do you know all the acronyms at your company? Or do you sometimes pretend you do because you don't want to appear stupid?

If you're a manager, what messages are you sending to your employees if you don't speak up when you don't understand something you think you're supposed to understand?

The unwritten rule becomes *don't ask questions which seem simplistic.* Of course, it's the simplistic question that often ends up being complicated.

If you don't know what an acronym means, it's likely someone else doesn't either. Or worse, people will have different interpretations or different meanings of the same acronym.

This leads to miscommunication, missed deadlines and general frustration.

As a manager or leader, if you have the confidence to ask what terms mean, you are helping others with understanding.

If we speak up when we don't know something we think everyone else knows:

- We find out what it means.
- We provide common ground and dialogue on specific terms.
- We are creating an environment where it's okay to speak up.

Often, basic information gets confused, which results in wasted time. Asking questions can help change that situation.

As a manager, have you ever had to own something you did which doesn't show you at your best?

You're an S.

Over 10 years ago, I was attending a very dry technical seminar. To make it worse, the instructor was more boring then the material. It was late in the day. We were all tired and very, very restless.

All of a sudden the instructor was talking about how to generate output from the computer. The way he described it was *getting the computer to take a dump*. He kept repeating *when you take a dump*.

Needless to say we tried to not laugh out loud. At first we were successful. We laughed quietly and smiled at each other. But the more he said *when you take a dump* the harder it became to refrain from laughing hysterically. It didn't take long before it was hard to breathe because we were laughing so hard.

The instructor never asked or understood what was funny.

Recently, I was teaching a management course and was covering the DiSC behavioral method. The conversations on this assessment are always different depending on the number of people in the workshop classified as D (dominant), or I (influence), or S (steady) or C (conscientious).

In this particular class I had one S (steady).

So I started to say *you're an S.*

I noticed a couple of people smiling and laughing. I asked what was funny. They told me. Up till then I didn't get what *you're an S* sounded like!

So I laughed.

And continued to use the phrase!

I could have been embarrassed or intimated if I viewed myself as the reason for the laugh. But as the group leader, I appreciated that I could contribute to the learning experience, albeit unintentionally, and connect with them in a different way.

As managers and leaders, when you accept and are okay with something that could make you look not your best:

- It sends a message to your team that you don't have to be perfect.
- It can bond you and your team in a different way.
- You help create an environment where alternative solutions, which might otherwise be missed, can be discovered.

And what you do might be remembered for a long time. You are a part of history!

I want them to want to be motivated to be on time!

There are many theories on motivation and how to motivate people in their job.

The bottom line, the commonality among all the theories, is that no one motivator works effectively for all people. What motivates one person can be different from what motivates another. Our responses to motivators stem from our backgrounds and our values.

Another truth common to all the theories is that money is NOT the biggest motivator.

If you think it is, ask yourself: *have you ever gotten a raise? Were you excited about the raise? And how long did the excitement last?* Most people say their excitement lasts from one minute to the first pay period, and then they take the raise for granted!!

This isn't to say people won't take other jobs for an increase in salary. It only means it will not sustain someone to stay in the job if it isn't meeting other conditions the person finds motivating.

A common trap for managers to fall into is motivating their employees to be on time.

Yes, there are certain employees who need to be at work at an exact time. It's a job requirement. We're not talking about those employees.

The majority of employees in a professional environment can have flexible start and end times for their work day.

The manager who focuses on employees who come in late is wasting their time as well as **DE-MOTIVATING** their employees. If they are not getting their work done focus on that. But the time issue is **YOUR** issue.

I had one manager who said *I want them <u>to want</u> to be motivated to be on time!*

An honest confession from a manager, and a statement we can all relate to – who doesn't want people to be motivated by what we are motivated by?

But unless we have the ability to mind alter and control people, it's not going to happen!

When you recognize that people aren't motivated by what you are motivated by:

- You can take the time to observe them to see what really does motivate them.
- You can ask them what motivates them and listen to what they say.
- You can continue to have conversations with them to understand their point of view.

When we let go of wanting others to be motivated by what motivates us, we allow the possibility for others to decide how they wish to be motivated.

The $64,000 Question

Do your questions lead to solutions, or to more problems?

Questions are extremely powerful. They can completely change the tone and direction of any conversation.

If the question is effective, it creates solutions and opportunities for issues that arise.

But if the question isn't effective, it can trap you in an abyss of problems!

I was coaching an executive who was stressed – he was based in Miami. It was a distinct possibility his site would close down and his employees would either have to move to the site in New Jersey or leave the company. (This story is not a joke about Jersey!) Most of his employees were Cuban so there was no way they would relocate.

His asked *"How can I keep their morale high when they know they might lose their jobs?"*

My response was quick – I said:

"I have no idea. If we do figure out the answer, let's write a book and get on Oprah!"

I think he was pretty surprised by this response – I mean, I was supposed to have the answer, right?! (Well not really, but he could have been thinking that!)

Then I said:

"I don't think that's a good question. There is no easy answer. Why don't we come up with a better question?"

Like what? (Now, that's a great question!)

So we brainstormed and changed the question to:

"How can I get my employees to continue to do their work while looking for other jobs?"

This question had answers. He was able to get into action.

That's the power and lesson about questions.

If you're coming up with bad answers, it's because the questions aren't good.

Change the question!

If you have trouble coming up with effective questions, a general rule is that the shorter the question, the greater chance for a different kind of answer. Shorter questions are less focused which means there could be more potential answers outside the realm of your possibility and perception! Examples of shorter questions include *What's next? What else? Like what?*

When we are in the midst of a lot of problems, with others or with ourselves:

- We can recognize we need to ask better questions to get better answers.
- We can keep the questions very basic.
- We can keep asking different questions until we come up with better answers.

How does that sound?

Dirt on the car

I was teaching a management course with managers from both the United States and other parts of the world.

We were discussing how to motivate people. One of the managers from another country said that to get his employee to work harder, he threw dirt on his car.

I thought it was a great metaphor.

Except that he literally meant it. He threw dirt on the guy's car!

This car is what the employee prized the most. The condition of the car was directly associated with his pride and esteem. So if he didn't meet expectations of the manager, the manager threw dirt on the car so it got dirty. This embarrassed the employee and he would change his actions to meet his manager's needs.

I don't suggest managers do this in the United States. HR might have just one or two concerns with this practice.

But what a brilliant concept!

It takes getting to know people in order to motivate them. Getting to know them means spending time with them on a regular basis, listening to them and asking questions in a space where they can feel safe answering questions.

This requires trust between both of you.

You can then motivate them either with rewards or punishment.

Rewards are preferable. Punishment can be necessary sometimes.

Is trust broken if you need to use punishment in order to get them to do something?

Maybe.

If you just throw dirt at them with no explanation, your actions will lead to broken trust.

But if you continue the conversations on a regular basis, they might see the dirt as necessary for their own good.

Which consequence would the employee rather have?

Have the dirt or be fired because he isn't doing his job?

In order for the punishment to be effective in the long run:

Make sure it's an action that really bothers the employee. When it is, the employee will want to do something to change it quickly. Continue your regular conversations to explain how the consequence could worsen over time if the behavior doesn't change now.
Allow the employee to vent, but not too much.

And then the dirt will start to turn to trust.

Questions, Jeopardy Style

Do you sometimes find yourself stuck no matter what questions you ask yourself?

One of the managers I coach attended a workshop where we went over the power of asking questions that lead to solutions.

So of course he knew how to ask questions that led to solutions!

So why was he stuck?

Come to think of it, I too know how to phrase questions that are powerful and have the potential to lead to strong solutions, and yet I sometimes get stuck as well.

When we are in the midst of a difficult task or situation, or when we have been doing something the same way for years, it can be difficult to break out of being stuck, even if we ask effective questions.

This is because we become too focused on the answer we have always gotten.

Whether you are dealing with a direct report who never seems to live up to her potential, or you are an entrepreneur attempting to expand your business and dealing with roadblocks; if you continue to focus on the answer you always got, it doesn't much matter what questions you ask!

So how about playing Jeopardy – start with the answer! (*Point of trivia – back in the 1960's, when Jeopardy was hosted by Art Fleming and* *the highest dollar value was $100 in double jeopardy, my mother was a contestant!*)

Instead of asking different questions, start with a different answer. Then come up with questions which will help get to the answer.

For example, if the manager continually has an issue with a direct report who always misses deadlines, she might have to ask questions such as *"What prevents you from getting the work done on time?"* Or, *"How can I support you so you get the work done on time?"*

But if this doesn't lead to any change, another possibility is to start with the answer!

Something like *prioritize my actions at the end of the day.*

Then the question might change to *"What time at the end of your day can you prioritize your next day actions?"* Or, *"What will take for you to prioritize the night before?"*

While this answer-question combination wouldn't be asked on Jeopardy, it does help you to formulate different questions when you are stuck.

When you start with the answer:

- You think about what outcomes you desire.
- You formulate actions to get to the outcomes.
- You base your questions on the outcomes or the actions.

Answer: Today

Question: When can I start formulating more effective question-answer combos!

The questions that lead nowhere

Why can't they do anything right?

Why is this project running late?

Why is it taking so long to fire them?

How can I do all the work I have to do when I'm always behind?

If you can come up with decent answers to any of these questions, let me know!

When managers ask these questions, they get frustrated. This is because there are no good answers to these questions. These are questions which lead to nowhere.

In a prior soundbite I mentioned the term focus vacuum. A vacuum is an empty space devoid of matter or devoid of solutions. Apply the word focus to this and it means focusing on this emptiness, focusing on empty space devoid of solutions.

Questions which lead to nowhere are focus vacuums. You are focusing on empty space devoid of solutions. This focus will continually lead you to frustration and stress.

But the good news: You can change the question to one that leads to solutions!

There are two general rules to shift these kinds of questions:

Don't start the question with the word *why*. *Why* usually puts people in a defensive position regarding something that isn't going well.

Don't keep asking yourself the same question if you don't get satisfactory answers!

Changing even a few words in a question could shift it from leading nowhere to leading to solutions.

Why can't they do anything right? can be changed to *What three things have they done well in the last six months?*

Why is this project running late? can be changed to *What can we do with this project right now?*

When you shift questions that lead nowhere to ones that have solutions:

You generate constructive, actionable steps.
You see alternatives.
You are less stressed!

What is one action you can take today to help solve a problem or resolve a situation? Go for it!!

What have I learned in 6 months of management?
Part 1 of 4

I asked one of the managers I was coaching what he learned in six months of re-focusing on management skills. Each response deserves its own soundbite, because they all incorporate skills managers should use to avoid traps and pitfalls.

The first answer written

Asking my managers to come up with their own solutions has proven to be effective much of the time.

Quite often you as a manager will try to do it all, including coming up with solutions for their employees. When they do this they are working too hard!

How will your employees grow if they don't start coming up with solutions, even if they aren't as good as what you would develop? How will they start to take ownership and more responsibility?

Yes, what they come up with might cause unnecessary detours. But they could also create solutions and alternatives you didn't think of yourself (yes, this is possible!).

Telling your employees instead of asking them to come up with solutions is about *control*. But when you tell them the solution and they don't do it exactly, how you explained it (or at least how you think you explained it) sets you up for stress and miscommunications. This is a trap you would want to avoid.

Allowing your employees to come up with their own solutions:

- Takes trust on your part and builds trust between the two of you
- Is a step towards more delegation
- Lets you focus on other employees and projects

Letting employees come up with solutions doesn't mean you can't be involved in the decision process. But you're including them as well.

Some managers don't realize this until they are working 60 to 80 hours a week and have had enough.

You can wait until you reach your breaking point or start now. The choice is yours!

What have I learned in 6 months of management?
Part 2 of 4

I asked one of the managers I was coaching what he learned in six months of re-focusing on management skills. Each response deserves its own soundbite, because they all incorporate skills managers should use to avoid traps and pitfalls.

The second answer written:

My employees seem to perform better when they believe I am watching what they're doing.

I didn't take this as a negative, that my client was micromanaging or managing by fear. Yes, there are managers who do these and it might work in the short term but it won't last. After all, *when the mice are away the cats will play*. At least if you lead by fear or micromanaging.

A successful manager has employees who work even when they aren't there.

I took my client's statement to mean when employees know their managers are watching, it shows the manager cares about what they do. They know their manager will be there to support them and help provide alternative solutions when needed.

What actions does a manager execute so an employee will know they care?

It can be listening more to them, talking to them, meeting with them regularly.

The underlying theme is taking *time*. Taking time when you think you don't have time.

When you manage to take time to manage:

- You have a better understanding of what each of your employees need from you
- You can be less reactive
- You show you care

And if you are performing as a manger, most employees want to perform as well.

What have I learned in 6 months of management?
Part 3 of 4

I asked one of the managers I was coaching what he learned in six months of re-focusing on management skills. Each response deserves its own soundbite, because they all incorporate skills managers should use to avoid traps and pitfalls.

The third answer written:

My staff seems to need and desire attention and appreciation.

Some employees want managers to leave them alone. Others want more guidance. Some employees want responsibility. Others seek direction.

But all of us want to know how we're doing. And we want to know this before we find out in an appraisal!

Have any of you been surprised come appraisal time? And I mean in a negative way? If you have, what happened? You probably felt de-motivated, angry, and the relationship suffered. It can take a long time to repair, or it may never get repaired, resulting in countless hours wasted in lost productivity and miscommunications.

Managers – you don't want your employees to answer *yes* to the above question!

One way to avoid surprises come appraisal time is by giving regular and ongoing feedback.

Regular and ongoing will be a different frequency for each of your employees. The ones who want to be left alone might have monthly or bi-monthly one on one sessions with you. The ones who need more direction will have more meetings with you, perhaps weekly.

Doing these meetings you have the opportunity to give feedback on what's working and what could be done differently. Your employee also has the opportunity to do the same.

During these meetings give them the attention and appreciation they desire and need.

When managers have regular meetings with their employees:

- There is an opportunity to correct work before it has to be negatively appraised
- They can motivate each of them by expressing how their work affects the company performance
- They are increasing trust between the two of you and you will be more successful as a manager!

Don't let *I don't have enough time to have these meetings* stop you from having these meetings. Make the time because ultimately it will save you time.

What have I learned in 6 months of management?
Part 4 of 4

I asked one of the managers I was coaching what he learned in six months of re-focusing on management skills. Each response deserves its own soundbite, because they all incorporate skills managers should use to avoid traps and pitfalls.

The fourth answer written:

Monthly meetings have proved to be an effective way to get feedback about what each employee needs to accomplish their goals.

I have asked hundreds of managers how often they meet one on one with their employees. The answers included *weekly, twice a month, monthly, when it's needed* and *they don't.*

For those managers who don't meet more frequently with their employees (and I'd say out of 100 managers, about 60% know they should meet more) the biggest excuse they give is there isn't enough time to meet with all their employees on a regular basis. They are too involved managing day to day operations or doing their own work.

This is one of the biggest manager traps!

Meeting with your employees should be one of your highest priorities. If there was ever something not to sacrifice due to time constraints, it's these meetings.

Why?

One on one meetings are the basis for achieving more effective management. The more feedback you give, the more comfortable you are giving it, the more comfortable others are hearing it and the more concise it can become.

Having these meetings helps you be proactive, potentially saving countless hours of productivity. It lessens the chance for miscommunications. It increases trust and a growing relationship between you and your employee.

A manager should meet with each employee weekly. This is ideal and many managers meet twice a month, or even once a month and experience the benefits.

Of course, the employee you wish to spend the least amount of time with is probably the employee you need to spend the most time with, potentially meeting daily for a period of time. This is one of the reasons a manager's job is challenging!

When you meet regularly with your employees:

- Your trust will increase which will make it easier to delegate
- You find out more about what motivates them
- You are increasing your success as an effective manager!

Manager's tools include *how to delegate effectively, how to coach successfully, increasing listening skills* and *how to give feedback which can be received in a positive manner.*

In order to do all this you need to create a space where using these tools will succeed.

This starts with taking the time, your time, to have one on one meetings.

Conclusion

I had one student in a workshop who announced that he had decided he didn't want to be a manager.

Good for him! (Now, if everyone in my class did this *I* would have a problem!)

Because he saw what skills are needed on a consistent basis to be an effective and successful manager, he decided he'd rather stay in a technical career track, and be an individual contributor. He saved himself from being unhappy, and he spared many others from the unhappiness of enduring his likely haphazard approach to being a manager.

I enjoy teaching skills to managers because there is never just one thing to learn or just one way to accomplish a task. Different people learn different things in different ways at different times.

What is important is for each participant to implement something. If you learn one new tool or the awareness to say something differently, you'll make a great start at reducing the complexity of your job as a manager.

All the traps and pitfalls I've written about, along with the tools for avoiding them, are connected and related. You can't motivate someone without asking questions. You can't give effective feedback if you don't have objective measurements. You can't give accurate performance appraisals without having ongoing, effective feedback sessions.

An accurate performance appraisal doesn't simply happen. It's the end result of work you do throughout the year, by meeting with your employees on a regular basis, providing effective feedback, and supporting them with their plan, not yours.

Feedback is vital for a strong manager-employee relationship. Knowing how to listen and how to ask questions to learn more about an employee is crucial. Using coaching skills can enhance opportunities for you to do this.

Delegating grows your employees and shows you trust them.

Management skills are very different from the technical skills required to perform other, non-management jobs. Skills that differentiate an excellent manager from a mediocre one include listening, asking questions, analyzing behavior (your own and others'), keeping agreements, and providing ongoing constructive feedback.

Just as technical skills require practice, it takes practice to make these management skills innate and natural to you. This is your job. When managers don't recognize this, they fall into many traps and pitfalls discussed in this book.

A large part of being a successful manager is to understand you – your values, preferences, motivators, weaknesses, and self-imposed obstacles. Sometimes it might seem like therapy when you analyze how your beliefs are helping you succeed or holding you back (and how does that make you feel?!).

One of the most powerful things you can do as a manager is to praise others. I end some of my workshops by having everyone sit in a circle. We begin the exercise by focusing on one person. Everyone else has a minute to say good things about that person. That person must sit and only listen. At the end, she can say two words – thank you. We proceed until every person has a turn.

This exercise usually produces more anxiety for everyone then anything else we did. That is until we are done. One woman argued with me about why we were doing this until we started and she saw the point of it. I had one man cry. Mostly, people see the impact they can have on others and they realize their significance.

As managers, you are all special people. You have the ability to help transform other people's lives. When you feel comfortable giving praise, focusing on the praise no matter who you are communicating it to, you are able to transcend, for that moment, any present conflict. You are avoiding the traps and pitfalls managers often make in that moment.

I hope for you many moments of avoiding the traps and pitfalls outlined in The Manager Trap.

There is enormous transformative power in your leadership role. If you can avoid the traps and pitfalls many managers continue to use, you will develop that power tremendously over time.

Resources

The following resources were referenced in some aspect in parts of the book:

- Mary-Kathryn Zachary, *Performance Evaluations Trigger Many Lawsuits* (*Supervision*, Page 23-26, Copyright (c) 2000, Bell & Howell Information and Learning Company.
- Bent Ericksen & Associates website, *Performance Appraisals*, by Frank Hotchkiss and Tim Twigg.
- http://www.all-acronyms.com
- http://wilderdom.com
- Beth Weissenberger for Handel Group
- Ken Blanchard's Situational Leadership II
- American Management Association's Time Management Workshop
- Tony Robbins RPM (Rapid Planning Method)

Howard Miller is an executive and business coach, trainer, and facilitator. He is available for keynote talks, one on one & group coaching, and meeting facilitation. He conducts management, team building and communication/behavioral skills workshops.

Howard teaches management skills to new managers, seasoned managers, entrepreneurs and executives. He uses his skills as a trainer, facilitator, and executive/management/business coach to help his clients utilize their internal behaviors and styles to maximize communication and productivity skills.

Howard's first book, *You're Full of Shift*, contains short stories which demonstrate shifting difficult situations into opportunities.

For further information, contact him at howard@fulcrumpointpartners.com.